REVOLUTIONARIES
FOR THE GOSPEL

Teófilo Cabestrero

REVOLUTIONARIES
FOR THE GOSPEL

Testimonies of Fifteen Christians
in the Nicaraguan Government

Translated from the Spanish by
Phillip Berryman

ORBIS BOOKS

Maryknoll, New York 10545

F
1528
.C3313
1986

The Catholic Foreign Mission Society of America (Maryknoll) recruits and trains people for overseas missionary service. Through Orbis Books Maryknoll aims to foster the international dialogue that is essential to mission. The books published, however, reflect the opinions of their authors and are not meant to represent the official position of the society.

Originally published as *Revolucionarios por el evangelio*, © 1983 by Desclée de Brouwer, Bilbao, Spain. The original edition has been edited for the Orbis translation

English translation © 1986 by Orbis Books, Maryknoll, NY 10545
All rights reserved
Manufactured in the United States of America

Manuscript editor: Mary Heffron
Spanish editor: Marianne Smith Varni

Library of Congress Cataloging in Publication Data

Cabestrero, Teófilo.
   Revolutionaries for the gospel.

   Translation of Revolucionarios por el evangelio.
   1. Nicaragua—History—Revolution, 1979—
Religious aspects.   2. Revolution (Theology).
3. Catholics—Nicaragua—Interviews.   4. Revolutionists—
Nicaragua—Interviews.   I. Title.
F1528.C3313   1986   972.85′05   85-25865
ISBN 0-88344-406-2 (pbk.)

CONTENTS

FOREWORD

Revolutionaries for the gospel

The title of this book is supremely fitting, although it may seem paradoxical to many people, maybe even shocking. These fifteen men and women of Nicaragua are revolutionaries. These fifteen men and women of Nicaragua are Christians. They are "revolutionaries for the gospel."

Anyone who reads this book with honesty will have to acknowledge that these people have taken on a double demand and are creating a single harmonious life, a life that they are publicly and consciously working out.

What these people understand by "revolution" is open to discussion, as is their way of interpreting the gospel. In fact, it would be a good idea for Christians and revolutionaries around the world to enter into discussion with revolutionary Christians in Nicaragua. Naturally these Nicaraguans should allow others the freedom they themselves are asking for in the church, the freedom Christ won for us once and for all.

I have read their testimony—frank, free, born of their experience—and I have no doubts about the gospel they live for, nor about the revolution they dream of and strive to serve in a gospel spirit. That does not mean that they can claim that theirs is the only legitimate interpretation of the gospel or the only legitimate interpretation of the revolution.

Serving the kingdom through effective love

With a journalist's skill and a missionary's concern, Teófilo Cabestrero has drawn out these fifteen professions of Christian faith and revolutionary commitment. I would like to highlight some common threads in the lives of these Christians, sometimes referring to their own words.

The only gospel these fifteen revolutionaries want is the gospel of our Lord Jesus Christ. Their program is "following Jesus": in this they are in tune with the early Christians and with all Christians who sincerely want to be disciples of Jesus. They go seeking the Holy Spirit. They pray every day, "up to an hour or more." They meditate on the Bible, they underline texts in it, and they share them in community with others. They take part in the Eucharist as the Passover of Jesus, who conquers death and transforms life. They may perhaps pray the rosary (like old Emilio, who had been a businessman). They have a knowledge of theology and an awareness of Christian spirituality. Almost all of them were schooled in the traditional kind of Catholic piety; they have taken part in evangelization movements in the church; they have studied the social doctrine of the church, and they know the difference between the magisterium and political opinions or interests that are not pastoral. They feel they are church, and specifically, the Catholic Church; they want to be church until they die even though it is hard and they are not always understood. For some of them, those who are older or who feel responsible for their children, the very idea that their children could one day cease being church is frightening. They profess their faith openly as Christians, and they want to evangelize temporal realities since those realities have eternal implications.

It is the gospel of Jesus that has pushed them into this arduous but magnificent effort. They are both pulled and pushed by the demands of the gospel, by Matthew 25, which tells us how we will all be judged one day by the standard of love, by whatever real love we have shown toward those real and specific brothers and sisters who were most in need.

They understand the revolution on the basis of the gospel and its demands. They have joined the revolution by a "Christian decision," and they define it critically as an instrument that is to be used at this particular moment in their country's history. Christian faith is their vital "motivation"; *Sandinismo* is their "instrument."

Revolution for them is not a matter of raising clenched fists and banners, of shouting revolutionary slogans and laying down floral wreaths. Nor do they see revolution as a turning everything upside-down. It is to serve, to carry out a transformation of society in response to the urgent needs and flagrant injustices in their country. For them it is Christian service to the kingdom of God. It is a service that is limited but inescapable; "creative" because it is Christian and revolutionary; borne up by the "boldness of the poor" and by that faith "which is greater than themselves" because it connects them with the very Spirit of God.

For these fifteen men and women becoming involved in the revolution, specifically the Sandinista people's revolution—and that is the one taking place in Nicaragua today—means taking on themselves the concrete service of loving their neighbor according to Jesus' commandment in a way that is real and effective today. For they have discovered that "neighbor" means not only your brother-in-law or someone in the neighborhood. For them loving one's neighbor is much more a matter of loving the people by serving the people—maybe "being reconciled with the people" if they were "exploiters of the people" before becoming revolutionaries, perhaps all the while considering themselves Christians. Now being Christian means working without making profit their aim, losing their social position, risking their own life or that of those they hold dear, devoting themselves to the welfare of the disinherited majorities, and accepting those broken relationships that the gospel announced, and that they now experience in a Nicaraguan way in their own flesh and blood and that of their family: as in the case, for example, of a daughter of one of Somoza's generals.

"Not everyone who says 'Lord, Lord' will enter into the kingdom," Jesus warned. These disciples of his in Nicaragua, "aspirants to being Christians and aspirants to being revolutionaries" have found their own translation of this text: not everyone who says " 'love, love' in the abstract" will enter the kingdom, but one who is committed with love to the creation of "new structures, new laws, new human beings"; one who is no longer willing to "keep in subjection those who have been subjected"; one who is willing to "help change the relations of production," not just to put on band-aids, but to strive to build up brotherly and sisterly relations; one who "works with love" and knows how to engage in "self-criticism" and humbly ask forgiveness.

These people are discovering, for themselves and possibly on behalf of many others, that true revolution must be true liberation. They are revolutionaries in the Sandinista people's revolution. They are Christians in the church because they are revolutionaries for the gospel, and they emphatically state: "We are revolutionaries because of the gospel and have no intention of setting up a church or organization parallel with the established church in Nicaragua."

Their testimony commits me as a Christian and as a bishop

I have read this book as a Christian and as a bishop—from the perspective of this moment in the life of this Latin America of ours, and from the perspective of our church, which is striving to live out the option for the poor.

As a Christian and as a bishop of the church of Jesus in Latin America, I will say that the confessions of these Nicaraguan men and women have moved me and demand commitment on my part. I find six reasons for this:

1. Their sense of church and their desire to be church forever—demanding, of course, the right to that freedom in the church which is theirs by the fact that they are baptized Christians; their Christian decision to take on coresponsibility as adults in the faith, without childishly bowing to the abuses that we "churchmen" all too often commit, whether by questionable teachings, or aggressive preaching, or pastoral impositions, or the way in which we administer the community's goods or present options in society or political commitments (which are always open to discussion since there must be plurality). They say correctly, "To be with the bishop does not mean to be with the bishop's politics," whatever the bishop's political stance might actually be.

2. Their evangelizing spirit and their committed missionary action; their generous decision to embody the gospel in the challenges of the new situation in Nicaragua today within the revolutionary process that is underway among the people—in order to be leaven in the mass and salt on the people's table.

They are living as Christians who know that their specific mission is to be involved, active, and committed in temporal realities. They know that this mission is recognized and praised in so many documents of the church's magisterium, which trusts the skill and capability of laypeople.

3. Their striking logic and utter docility to the Spirit, which they try to translate into real life. They are thus discovering those essential ideas of the

gospel such as "voluntary self-impoverishment" and abnegation so as to share in a brotherly and sisterly way with the poor and impoverished majority in their country, plundered as it has been for centuries. With a logion worthy of Jesus the teacher they declare that "happiness lies not in what you have, but in what you give."

4. Their understanding that the option for the poor has to be something that can be verified politically, economically, and socially, expressed in works of justice in the community, in giving up class privileges, and in doing what clearly benefits the poor majority. That option cannot be limited to the church in the Third World. I too am convinced that "being identified with the struggle of the poor is a universal calling of the church," assuming that it wants to be the church of Jesus of Nazareth.

5. Their passionate involvement with Jesus Christ as a person, their basic aim of walking along with the "following of Jesus." They want to make that following—which for them is made concrete in their beloved Nicaragua as it strives to become something new—the Christian spirituality of the new men and women of Nicaragua and of the Americas. Humbly, as disciples, they even ask that some Latin American Ignatius Loyola open up paths for such a Latin American Christian spirituality all over their continent.

For my part, I state, simply but firmly, that this book of interviews will become indispensable for the task of formulating, out of experience, that gospel spirituality of liberation toward which the Spirit of Jesus is calling us so strongly.

6. These people do not flee from the cross of Christ. They take on contradictions in the hope of clarifying them in the light of the gospel, remaining faithful to a process that is certainly relative but that they can no more avoid than they can avoid living in history. In the hope of the kingdom and in service to the church these people endeavor to raise to a higher level those deep divisions that they suffer in their families and in the community of the church. Since they have been the companions of martyrs, they do not shun the call to martyrdom.

I am not canonizing these fifteen men and women

I am not canonizing these fifteen men and women, Christians and revolutionaries, Nicaraguans and Sandinistas. It is not a good idea to canonize people who are still wandering around on this earth where things are still so contingent. They themselves point out their own limitations and personal faults and they recognize failings, errors, and limitations in the Nicaraguan revolutionary process, the Sandinista revolution.

As Christians and revolutionaries, they must always be free and faithful— more clearsighted and faithful each day, free in their self-criticism and in their committed criticism both of the church and of the revolution in which they are working through their service to the people.

Their God, their people, and all of us who share their hope, will hold them accountable, in the name of history and of the kingdom, if they fail to keep the solemn oath that several of them swear in their interviews in such a Christian manner: "The day this revolution is not serving the welfare of the poor majority, we will be the first to criticize it."

A Christian should be new every day, just like the utterly new Good News of Jesus. A revolutionary must carry out the revolution each day—and that means in society, in the family, and in one's own heart, which ever tends to grow old.

Here you will find fifteen testimonies written down, but there are many thousands of other, living testimonies in Nicaragua. Thousands of men, women, and children, Christians and revolutionaries, freely and sacrificially, are taking part in building the kingdom at this dramatic moment in Central America and in all Latin America. Many do not understand them; the light of dawn is never completely clear. The light of liberation will become clearer—not without doubts, not without risks, not without problems—in history and in the church.

I want to thank these fifteen "confessors" of the faith and of political struggle for their moving testimony. And I want to give thanks to this tiny Nicaragua and to the church that has produced them. Most of all I want to give thanks to the God and Father of our Lord Jesus Christ, who never ceases to pour forth his Spirit to renew the face of the earth and the countenance of his people.

Christians and revolutionaries, these witnesses are also poets, witnesses of a word that is militant. They "want to die facing away from the night," since the gospel impels them to believe that "the Day is far advanced."

I join them in their hope.

PEDRO CASALDÁLIGA
BISHOP OF SÃO FÉLIX DO ARAGUAIA
MATO GROSSO, BRAZIL

PREFACE

It is common knowledge that several priests are members of the Nicaraguan revolutionary government. That fact has become a matter of controversy.* But few people are aware that more than thirty Christian laypeople who practice their faith hold high positions in that same revolutionary government.

In these pages fifteen of these Christians, men and women, explain their twofold identity, their twofold militancy, and their twofold hope, Christian and revolutionary. Among them are cabinet ministers, vice-ministers, directors general, secretaries general, court presidents.

In the spiritual and political journeys of these Nicaraguan Christians, the reader will find details of their origins, their schooling, the changes and struggles they have experienced leading up to their present convictions. The reader will see their aspirations relating to the gospel and society and their hopes, both well-reasoned and utopian.

The testimonies offered here are not dogmas of faith but experiences lived within the process of a people, a people that is poor and has been held in subjection, most of whom are Christians. These interviews should be approached openly. We should shake ourselves free of preconceptions (pro or con) resulting from opinions we might have held previously and unquestionably. We should receive testimonies with an honest freedom that leaves an area of trust and openness, as persons really listening to other persons. After listening, let us judge with critical freedom, as befits people who are also to be judged.

I am grateful to the people interviewed here, and I take my cue from them. May they be true revolutionaries and true Christians: neither baptizing the revolution with their faith nor prostituting their faith for the revolution (fanaticizing neither the revolution nor the faith). No such utilization is justified simply because others utilize the faith—overtly or subtly—against the people's revolution.

For these fifteen men and women, for all who try to be both Christians and revolutionaries (and for all Christians—why not?) my brotherly wish is that we be wholehearted in our fidelity:

---

*See Teófilo Cabestrero, *Ministers of God, Ministers of the People: Interviews with Three Priests in the Government of Nicaragua* (Maryknoll, N.Y.: Orbis Books, 1983).

• faithful to the faith; faithful to the God of Jesus Christ and to the gospel of the kingdom; faithful to the church (to the people of God with the hierarchy, and to the hierarchy with the people of God).

• faithful to the people; faithful to the revolutionary process among the people, so that the process may faithfully serve the true common good of the people.

• faithful always to the most humble, the most disinherited and the poorest. This fidelity combines all other fidelities, for they, the poor, are the suffering heart of the people's hope; they are the wounded face of Christ; and they are the glorious future of the church because in the design of God they are the privileged ones of the kingdom.

May these pages serve to bring such fidelities together: to bring brothers and sisters together; to sow the seeds of the gospel and of hope; to unite people of good will and love; to dispel fear and enlighten consciences, communities, churches; to liberate peoples; to build the kingdom.

Whatever be the future course of the people's revolution in Nicaragua, and of the aggressive actions of its enemies, may these interview-testimonies stand as signs or roadmarks, as seeds in history, for churches and peoples.

ACRONYMS

AMNLAE   Asociación de Mujeres Nicaragüenses Luisa Amanda Espinosa (Luisa Amanda Espinoza Association of Nicaraguan Women)

AMPRONAC   Asociación de Mujeres ante la Problemática Nacional (Association of Nicaraguan Women to Deal with National Problems)

ARDE   Alianza Revolucionaria Democrática (Democratic Revolutionary Alliance); the coalition of contras originally allied with Edén Pastora and based in Costa Rica. Pastora was expelled by ARDE's leaders in May 1984 and the group agreed to unite with the FDN.

ATC   Asociación de Trabajadores del Campo (Association of Rural Workers)

CDS   Comités de Defensa Sandinista (Sandinista Defense Committees); replacing the CDC after victory; assumed local responsibility for the tasks of reconstruction and defense

CEPA   Centro de Educación y Promoción Agrícola (Agricultural Promotion Education Center); church-related training center for peasant leaders

CONDECA   Consejo de Defensa Centroamericano (Council for Central American Defense); a creation of the Inter-American Defense Board, Washington, D.C.

CPDH   Comision Permanente de Derechos Humanos (Permanent Commission on Human Rights)

CSN   Coordinadora Sindical de Nicaragua (Coordinating Body of Unions of Nicaragua)

CSUCA   Consejo Superior Universitario Centroamericano (Confederation of Central American Universities, Costa Rica)

ENALUF   Empresa Nacional de Luz y Fuerza (National Light and Power; pre-victory)

FAO   Frente Amplio de Oposición (Board Opposition Front); upper-class political coalition that opposed Somoza but sought a modified status quo

FSLN   Frente Sandinista de Liberación Nacional (Sandinista Front for National Liberation)

xv

GPP	Guerra Popular Prolongada (Prolonged People's War); tendency in FSLN
INE	Instituto Nicaragüense de Energía (Nicaraguan Energy Institute)
IRENA	Instituto de Recursos Naturales (Nicaraguan Institute for National Resources)
MPU	Movimiento Pueblo Unido (United People's Movement); a broad-based popular front organization of the FSLN
PPSC	Partido Popular Social Cristiano (Popular Social Christian Party)
UDEL	Union Democrática de Liberación (Democratic Union for Liberation); a liberal alternative political coalition that opposed Somoza; led by Pedro Joaquín Chamorro
UNAP	Unión Nacional de Acción Popular (National Union of People's Action)
UNO	Unión Nacional Opositora (National Opposition Union)

CHRONOLOGY

1522–24	Nicaragua colonized by Spain.
1811	First armed rebellion against Spain.
1854	U.S. forces invade Nicaragua, destroying San Juan del Norte, to avenge an insult to the American minister to Nicaragua.
1857	U.S. citizen William Walker attempts to gain control of Nicaragua. U.S. troops invade to protect American interests several times between 1857 and 1911. Conservative Party rules Nicaragua; presidents change every 4 years until 1893.
1912	U.S. marines protect American interests during civil war. A force remains until August 5, 1925.
1926	U.S. marines invade following coup d'etat of General Chamorro and renewed civil war. Their work includes activity against the leader General Augusto César Sandino and they remain in the country until 1933.
1933	Elections bring Liberal Juan Sacasa to the presidency. North American troops leave Nicaragua after long guerrilla war led by General Augusto César Sandino's forces. U.S. leaves behind a legally constituted and fully trained National Guard under the leadership of Anastasio Somoza García. Following withdrawal of Americans, Somoza negotiates a peace between Sandino and President Sacasa.
1934	(Feb. 21) After attending a dinner at the presidential palace, Sandino is arrested on Somoza's order and executed.
1936	Somoza García comes into power after a coup d'etat against President Sacasa.
1940	(Nov. 27) Pedro Hurtado, uncle of Roberto Argüello, now president of the Supreme Court, is arrested and tortured by Somoza's agents.
mid-1940s	Liberals form the Independent Liberal Party, which, with the Conservative Party, subsequently form the opposition to the Somoza dictatorship.
1946	Reinaldo Tefel starts a weekly "Sandinista" paper, *El Universitario*. Tefel is exiled to Mexico.

1954	Nicaragua assists U.S. in its invasion of Guatemala.
1956	(Sept. 21) Anastasio Somoza García is killed by poet and patriot Rigoberto López Pérez. Luis Somoza Debayle, Anastasio's eldest son, assumes control with the support of the U.S. Anastasio II (Tachito) Somoza Debayle heads National Guard. Repression of opposition and imprisonment and torture of all suspected to be involved in the assassination.
1959	Cuban Revolution.
	Uprising in Nicaragua led by Enrique Lacayo Farfán, Independent Liberal, and Pedro Joaquín Chamorro, editor of *La Prensa*, fails. Miguel Ernesto Vijil, now Minister of Housing, participates.
1960s	Somoza's power becomes entrenched through pacts with other leaders, accumulation of family assets, links with North American capital, and close associations with Central American bourgeoisie.
1961	U.S. sets up Alliance for Progress.
	U.S.-backed invasion of Cuba defeated at Playa Giron (Bay of Pigs). Nicaragua is used as a training base and launching pad for the invasion.
	(July 26) Sandinista Front for National Liberation (FSLN) founded in Honduras by Carlos Fonseca Amador, Tomás Borge, and Silvio Mayorga.
1962–65	Second Vatican Council.
1963	FSLN allies with Nicaraguan Socialist Party and Republican Mobilization Organization.
1964	Somoza and U.S. bring about the formation of CONDECA to coordinate counterinsurgency in Central America.
1965	Nicaraguan National Guard assists in U.S. intervention in Dominican Republic.
1967	Anastasio Somoza Debayle becomes president following the death of his brother Luis from a heart attack.
	Left parties join Liberals and Conservatives in electoral politics. FSLN breaks from alliance. First military action takes place in Pancasán. FSLN retreats to mountains, begins underground organizing.
	(Oct.) Che Guevara is killed in Bolivia.
1968	Latin American Episcopal Conference meets in Medellín (Colombia) to apply the concepts of Vatican II to the Latin American church.
	Capuchin priests in Zelaya create the first course for lay ministers and local community leaders, "Delegates of the Word."

1968–70	Christian base communities develop in poor areas of Managua and other cities.
1969	Agrarian Promotion and Education Center (CEPA) founded by the Jesuits. CEPA and "Delegates of the Word" attempt to integrate biblical reflection and technical agricultural training among people in the countryside.
1970–72	Growing political opposition to Somoza by non-Marxist political elites. César Delgadillo with others collect signatures petitioning government for structural change. People occupy churches throughout the country. Somoza agrees to political reforms and new election law with interim junta.
1971–72	Triumvirate junta ("Junta of the Three Little Pigs") arranged by Somoza in response to popular protest against government. Somoza terminates the junta after the December 1972 earthquake.
1972	(Dec.) Earthquake destroys a large part of Managua. Economy is stimulated because of influx of international public and private funds for reconstruction, insurance, and favorable prices for exports (sugar, beef, and coffee). People's needs are not responded to, however, precipitating a radicalization of the people of all classes.
	Archbishop Miguel Obando y Bravo publicly criticizes Somoza's government and calls for a "new order."
1972–74	Somoza rules by decree. Family and cronies profit from reconstruction and graft.
1974	FSLN begins major military action with an attack on the house of Somoza's Minister of Agriculture; holds hostages for 60 hours and wins major demands. National Guard begins massacres and repression attempting to crush popular support for Sandinistas.
	(Dec.) Democratic Union of Liberation (UDEL) formed as united opposition front. Led by Pedro Joaquín Chamorro.
1974–77	Martial law and press censorship in effect.
1975	Tendencies develop in FSLN: Guerra Popular Prolongada (GPP), who believed in the need for a permanent military base in the mountains to fight a prolonged war; the Proletarian (TP), who believed the working class should be the base. In late 1975 the GPP sanctions the Proletarian tendency.
1976	(Winter) A third tendency develops in exile: the Insurrectionalists, who felt that Somoza was inherently weak and who wanted attacks against the National Guard from outside Nicaragua.

Committee of Agricultural Workers leads land invasions and protest marches.

Capuchin priests denounce mass murders and tortures of peasants in northern Nicaragua.

(Nov.) FSLN founder Carlos Fonseca Amador killed.

(Winter) CONDECA forces supposedly eliminate FSLN during training operations.

1977–79 Nicaragua's Conference of Bishops, led by Archbishop Obando y Bravo of Managua, produces a series of pastoral letters denouncing the dictatorship and supporting the people's right to struggle.

1977 Somoza lifts state of siege in effect since 1974 to counter negative rumors and under pressure from U.S.

(July) Somoza suffers heart attack.

(Sept. 29) Association of Nicaraguan Women to Deal with National Problems (AMPRONAC) organized. Teresa Cardenal and Zela Díaz founding members.

Association of Rural Workers (ATC) formed by Sandinistas.

(Oct.) Insurrectionalist guerrillas attack National Guard barracks in Ocotal and San Carlos, Masaya and Managua. Attempt to take over the whole country is not successful. Communiqué from the Twelve (in Costa Rica) calls on population to work with Sandinista Front.

María del Socorro Gutiérrez's brother is imprisoned.

(Oct. 26) Permanent Commission for Human Rights (CPDH) founded.

(Oct.–Nov.) CPDH, AMPRONAC, and student groups protest the disappearance of hundreds of campesinos.

Mass movement against Somoza picks up momentum.

1978 (Jan. 10) Pedro Joaquín Chamorro, publisher and editor of opposition paper *La Prensa*, assassinated after publishing UDEL's demands regarding human rights. His death unites opposition; riots and general strike follow.

(Jan. 22) "General Strike for Justice" supported by non-Somoza-controlled bourgeoisie and entire trade union movement.

(Feb.) Monimbó uprising. National Guard begins aerial bombardment of defiant barrio.

(July 17) Twenty popular organizations organize the United People's Movement (MPU) to devise a moderate bourgeois alternative to Somoza. Support from Carter administration. Exodus of bourgeois class from country. Sandinista Front becomes leader of the people.

(July) The Twelve return from exile in Costa Rica and are greeted by huge popular demonstrations. They endorse the FSLN, though most are in sympathy with Terceristas. Petty bourgeoisie flock to ranks of Terceristas.

(Aug. 22) FSLN attacks the National Palace in Managua (Nicaragua's Congress), winning freedom for political prisoners and other demands.

General strike, except for banking sector.

(Sept.) Insurrection in 7 cities is put down by the National Guard. Repression and bombing of markets and other civilian areas follow.

(Sept.) General Edmundo Menesis, father of Vidaluz Meneses, now Director of Libraries and Archives, is fatally wounded in Guatemala, where he had been Somoza's ambassador.

1979   The three tendencies of the FSLN announce organic unity.

(May 29) First united FSLN offensive begins in southern Nicaragua.

(June) Sandinistas form a provisional government in Costa Rica.

(July 17) Somoza flees to Miami.

(July 19) National Guard surrenders. FSLN enters Managua.

The Government of National Reconstruction based on an alliance including sectors of the bourgeoisie is set up.

(Fall) Agrarian Reform begins.

1980   (March) Literacy Crusade is launched.

(Oct.) FSLN issues statement on religion promising total freedom and asserting right of Christians to membership in FSLN. Nicaraguan Episcopal Conference responds with a pastoral letter denouncing materialist ideologies in Nicaragua.

1980–83   Tension develops between hierarchy and popular movement in Nicaragua. Archbishop Obando y Bravo removes some priests sympathetic to the government from their parishes. Parishioners of Santa Rosa who protest the loss of their pastor are excommunicated by the archbishop.

1981   (Jan.) U.S. suspends economic aid to Nicaragua.

(Oct.) Second phase of Agrarian Reform.

(Nov.) President Reagan secretly approves military aid to anti-Sandinista forces (contras). Contras trained in Florida in violation of U.S. law.

1982   (March) U.S. covert aid program becomes public.

(April) Eden Pastora (in Costa Rica) declares his determination to overthrow the Sandinista government.

(August) U.S. and Honduras hold joint military maneuvers. U.S. builds and expands airstrips in Honduras.

(Sept.) Eden Pastora joins with Alfonso Robelo and Brooklyn Rivera to form counterrevolutionary organization ARDE.

1983 (Jan.) Mexico, Venezuela, Panama, and Colombia meet on Contadora Island to discuss diplomatic proposals for peace in Central America. Thus the Contadora regional peace effort is launched, the four countries stating that the East-West context is inappropriate for resolving the crisis.

(Feb.) U.S. and Honduras hold Big Pine I maneuvers in Honduras near Nicaraguan border.

(March) Pope John Paul II visits Nicaragua. Pope responds to a crowd chanting, "We want peace!" by angrily shouting, "Silence!" His speeches on Catholic education and unity around bishops interpreted as against revolution. He reproves Ernesto Cardenal.

(April) Pastora and ARDE begin armed attacks into Nicaragua.

(Nov. 9) Restoration of dialogue between Nicaraguan Bishops Conference and government.

(Nov.) U.S. Congress provides contras with $24 million.

(Dec.) Nicaraguan government declares amnesty for Miskito Indians and campesinos involved with armed counter-revolutionary forces. Control loosened on national press.

1984 (April) CIA assists contras in mining Nicaraguan harbors.

(Easter Sunday) Pastoral Letter from Nicaraguan bishops calls for reconciliation of all Nicaraguans, but does not mention recent elections, continued contra attacks, or U.S. mining of harbors. Provokes formal break between bishops and government.

(June) U.S. Secretary of State Shultz meets Nicaraguan leader Daniel Ortega in Managua. Talks begin.

(July) Archbishop Obando and 15–20 priests lead an antigovernment march. Ten foreign priests are deported as a result.

(Sept.) Nicaragua agrees to sign Contadora pact. U.S. urges its allies in the region to demand changes in text of the treaty.

(Oct.) CIA manual telling contras how to "neutralize" Nicaraguan officials made public.

(Nov. 4) National elections held. Daniel Ortega Saavedra elected president.

1985 (Jan.) U.S. breaks off bilateral talks with Nicaragua, withdraws from World Court jurisdiction.

(Feb.–May) Big Pine III joint U.S.-Honduras military maneuvers.

(April) President Reagan asks for $14 million in aid to contras, proposes cease-fire and talks. Aid fails in Congress.

Archbishop Obando named cardinal.

(May) U.S. declares trade embargo.

(June) Angered at President Ortega's trip to the USSR, Congress approves $27 million in "nonlethal" military aid to contras.

(July) Miguel d'Escoto resigns temporarily from foreign ministry and fasts 27 days to dramatize Nicaragua's efforts for peace, to denounce U.S. "terrorism," and to call for an "evangelical insurrection" for peace.

(Oct.) Copies of new archdiocesan paper confiscated. Nicaragua declares state of emergency and suspends civil liberties for one year.

1

ROBERTO ARGÜELLO

President of the Supreme Court

"It is my search for justice and my Christian principles that have made me a revolutionary"

Robert Argüello was born in Granada (Nicaragua) November 2, 1930. In 1955 he received a doctorate in law from the National University of Nicaragua (León); he practiced law until 1979 and had a reputation for defending political prisoners. He is married to María del Socorro Leiva. They have four children.

In 1977 Argüello joined the group known as the Twelve.* After the revolutionary victory he became president of the Supreme Court.

●

Argüello postponed our interview several times because of his work, emergencies, trips outside the country with government delegations. Finally, one day, he comes to my house at the parish in Las Palmas at five in the afternooon, after his office hours. He arrives thirsty and hot. I give him some pitaya *juice from the refrigerator. We sit down face to face in a small parlor with a tape recorder between us. This man is stocky and speaks with a strong, firm voice.*

> We've had to create a new judicial system—one that is more just than the previous one—to create structures, laws, and people educated in the law.

Argüello—The courts all disappeared along with the old government. Not only the courts but the whole system of public order—the president, the ministers, all members of congress, all the senators, all the police, the whole army. There was not even a single member of the judicial branch left. Our job has been huge: to organize a new judicial system as we went along, aiming to make it different from the previous one. But we face many problems. You can't fix rotten structures overnight, just with a decree.

Our first job was to gradually get civil power back from the hands of the Sandinista Army, which had occupied all the towns and every corner of Nicaragua. The army was handling legal matters where it had taken over because at that time there were no authorities. The only authorities were the guerrillas who had taken the town. We had to look for responsible people, honest people. We put honesty above schooling, since we didn't have enough judges with experience. At that time, especially at the municipal level, it was very hard to find people trained to administer justice. Judges were appointed, and little by little the system was taken back from the military, from the hands of armed guerrillas.

We had to convince those guerrillas to hand over power to civil judges, lay judges, at the municipal level, and to accept the dictates of these lay judges in

---

*The Twelve was a group of highly respected Nicaraguans, businessmen, professionals, and priests, who publicly opposed the dictatorship from October 1977 onwards. Since the mid-1970s there had been opposition from political parties and especially the UDEL (Democratic Union for Liberation) coalition, but the Twelve was the first group to publicly recognize the Sandinistas as a positive force.

their jurisdiction. At first we had many problems. There was no way to make people obey a judge in the provinces and in small villages. At the same time the police force was being organized, and both were learning together, the judge in relation to the police, and the police in relation to the judge. Little by little the rough spots were smoothed over.

We also had conflicts because some of the judges we appointed were rejected by the people of the area. There were run-ins with the popular organizations, the mass organizations. In several cases, these organizations occupied courtrooms to protest the appointments. That created a series of problems. We couldn't send in the police to get the people out of the courtroom. At the moment of victory of a revolution like this one we had to find a way to persuade them. Solutions were found in each case. Finally the people realized that no court or tribunal should be taken by violence or force, but rather that any protest or complaint against a judge should be channeled through the normal legal process, and that it would have to be proven that the person was acting wrongly. Many of the complaints against judges turned out to be unfounded, due to political rivalry, cronyism, rumors, or backbiting.

It took us nine months, more or less, to organize the judicial branch in Nicaragua. And then we realized that this judicial system had the same faults as the previous one—and still has. The Supreme Court reasoned that the problem started at the local level, and so we set up a training program for forty young people who are preparing to be municipal judges in their provinces. The basic problem is education. We lack people trained and prepared to administer justice. We have begun to correct this and we are also dealing with the conflicts that arise because of our old laws. We have laws dating from the last century that do not fit the present revolutionary situation. The incongruities crop up all the time, especially regarding land and rental, and there are thorny questions every day. Police sometimes don't obey a judge's orders—for example, when they see a judge order a criminal set free for lack of proof. The police may be quite unhappy if they have spent many days and nights catching that criminal.

These are the kinds of structural problems we've had to solve as we go along. Not only are we lacking the kinds of laws we need to deal with them, but we don't have the people with legal training to apply the laws.

Q—Structures, laws, people. Is the revolution creating new laws?

—The revolution is often ahead of the laws. The revolution creates situations that get ahead of existing laws and often render those laws ineffective. That happens every day. For example, there have been occupations of uncultivated land. The people took those lands to plant crops—they needed land. That is what the revolution is all about, land, land for the person who works it.

The civil Code of Nicaragua contained laws that would have made it possible to have those people thrown off the land; a court order could have forced them off the land. That was not an individual problem, however, but a social problem. It is one thing to evict a person who has taken over a house by force, and another thing to evict a whole group of peasants who out of their need have occupied lands in order to plant crops so they can eat—even though the law correctly says that you cannot occupy a piece of land or a farm.

The point was not just to make a strict application of the law from an individual standpoint—for example, to send the police after a group that was occupying land—but to provide a social solution in cases like this. As a result Agrarian Reform was speeded up. Now peasant claims are channeled through the Agrarian Reform and peasants are being given land. So land occupations have ceased. But our judges got stuck in problems because the old law didn't allow such things. The revolution had to respond by creating the Agrarian Reform Law. Land problems could not be solved in the courts. What impact could a judge's court decision have when a whole townful of people had occupied a farm—especially in the immediate postrevolutionary period?

—Is the revolution going to be ahead of the law for a long time? Is it going to take a long time for the body of law to catch up to the revolution?

—Our laws are very old. I think it will take a long time to reform the laws. You cannot change all a country's structures at one stroke; some of them have to remain. The main thing we are doing is pushing forward an institutional reform of our legislation on penal processes and on how the courts should be organized in order to streamline the process, to expedite it, so court procedures won't be stretched out with all the harm that means for individual freedom. We also intend to cut costs.

Another basic problem is how to bring it about that people will feel represented by their judges. We are trying to find a way whereby the people will feel that the judges are theirs, and not that they simply represent a particular class, as was the case before, when judges showed no respect for the people, and in fact were not really judges at all, but representatives of a social system and of a class.

The change must be deep and structural, because we cannot be simply applying band-aids or improvising reforms, leaving the evil still there. On the economic side, we need buildings, supplies, transportation—and laboratories, an institute for forensic medicine for autopsies. In this whole area we are working with very primitive means. The problem of justice is not as easy as people might think. It is not just a question of changing laws; acquiring the means for carrying out justice and a budget for undertaking planned solutions are also important. Some municipal courts in Nicaragua have a dirt floor, and the judge's platform has only a clean table, a stool, and a pencil, maybe not even paper.

—Have you been president of the Supreme Court since the revolutionary victory?

—Yes. The way I was appointed was quite unusual. All of us on the court began at the same time. We were appointed without any consultation, through a decree while the war was still going on. I found out I had been made a magistrate by short-wave radio, when it was announced that the revolution had set up a new Supreme Court, a Supreme Court "in arms." That automatically put us at odds with the law, so I immediately had to take security measures.

Right after the revolutionary victory, we were sworn in, and since that moment we have been working with the revolution. The money aspect is not of concern: each of us used to earn more in our law offices than we do today, since there is a limit of 10,000 cordobas a month for public servants, and we could still earn more in private practice today. [By the official exchange rate 10,000 cordobas would be U.S. $1,000; by the (legal) parallel rate about U.S. $350, and by the black market rate far less.—TRANS.]

As a lawyer I worked all the time. I worked on civil and commercial law cases, although I was very interested in defending the human rights of political prisoners. I took part in many important cases in Nicaragua; I defended Dr. Pedro Joaquín Chamorro, for example. His martyrdom had a great impact on me. I also took cases in military courts. During the last military courts, over a hundred *muchachos* of the Sandinista Front were put on trial. I handled the defense for several of them. As their defense lawyer, I prophesied before the military court that those who were found guilty today would govern tomorrow. That prophecy has been fulfilled: many members of the government today had been sentenced to a hundred years in prison. History is amazing!

—*How did the Sandinistas strike you when you were serving as their defense lawyer?*

—For me it was like a laboratory, since I came into contact with people whose thinking was different from mine. I came to realize that there was another version of history, not just of the story of Sandino but of all Nicaraguan history. I was especially impressed by one very bright professor who was sentenced in a military court, Professor Iván Montenegro Báez, who was later killed in the war. He had a clear vision of history and we had long conversations. His analysis made me realize that what I had learned was not the real history of Nicaragua. From that point on, I gradually came closer to the Sandinista group, until I was practically a sympathizer. No one else wanted to take their cases, and when I did I was criticized by my other clients. In fact I lost a lot of clients. They looked at me as though I were a communist.

My father was imprisoned and an uncle of mine was tortured. This pushed me into the struggle against the Somoza regime.

—*What impelled you to defend the Sandinistas?*

—I had always admired any people who were political prisoners. My first case, that of Lesbia Carrasquilla, made a great impression on me. Her husband (now Captain) Roberto Sánchez, who had been a student in my penal law class, came to my house to tell me no one wanted to take his wife's case, and he asked me to defend her. I said, "I'll take her case for you." And in fact I was able to get Lesbia Carrasquilla, who had been tortured, out of jail. That is how I began defending political prisoners.

I gained a lot of experience in political cases, in human rights cases, and in the cases of those making human rights protests. I belonged to organizations for human rights and became specialized in human rights cases. Now that I am in the government I can continue to do that. I am well aware of what is involved in human rights, and we are very insistent that human rights must be respected. The Supreme Court has intervened in many cases, or I have done so personally.

Among the things that impelled me in my profession to join the struggle against the Somoza regime and its injustice were the prison terms my father suffered under Somoza and the fact that an uncle of mine, Dr. Pedro Hurtado, was tortured. He wrote a pamphlet, something that was very dangerous at the time, a pamphlet on his own torture, "Torture as a System." That is one of the main reasons I became involved in the struggle for human rights and against the daily injustice that occurred in Nicaragua. I have been involved since shortly after my graduation in 1955.

—*I'd like to explore another aspect of your life. Are you a Christian?*

—Yes, I'm a Christian. I have an absolute faith in God. I went to Catholic schools all my life. My convictions are strong, even though I don't belong to groups or sects. I don't belong to organizations of cursillistas or charismatics, but I'm a Christian with strong convictions.

My parents were Christians, practicing Catholics, and they instilled religion in us. In my family we are all Christians, Catholics. My brother Alvaro is a Jesuit, and has represented the Nicaraguan clergy in the Council of State.

—*Did your Christian faith influence your political involvement and your struggle on behalf of political prisoners?*

—I think so, especially in this search one makes, the personal search for justice, this desire to find justice in the full sense. The death of my brother Gustavo in Somoza's jail was a terrible blow, but it strengthened my spirit even more. He was arrested on September 9, 1978, and his body was handed over on September 12, three days after the arrest. He had been beaten and tortured, along with the other *muchachos* whose convictions had put them alongside their people in the 1978 insurrection, which was led by the Sandinista National Liberation Front.

—*Do you pray, do you personally turn to God?*

—Naturally. I always entrust myself to God in my prayers and I feel that prayer gives me life and energy. I don't go around showing off my Christianity, and I don't participate in any Christian group. In that sense I am an isolated Christian, I'm quite free about that. My wife and my children are also Christian and enthusiastically involved in the revolution.

As I see it, this revolution meshes very well with Christianity, especially insofar as it aims to benefit the poor and favors the most marginal groups in the country. Everything the revolution has done has been for the poor at the expense of those who are better off. That's where I see a great deal of overlap between the revolution and Christianity, in the love the gospel shows toward workers, the humble people.

—*Don't you also see some points of contrast, conflict, opposition, between the revolution and Christianity?*

—Not between the revolution and Christianity. I see the conflict with certain ministers of religion, certain bishops, who, as I see it, have not been able to understand this era we are living in. Their thinking has not caught up and they don't understand the change that is going on in society. They want to apply an obsolete framework to this moment in history.

—*And the accusations leveled at the Sandinista revolution, that it is persecuting the church and religion in order to set up an atheistic Marxist-Leninist regime in Nicaragua?*

—This whole thing is blown out of proportion, and there is a good deal of calumny in it, for political purposes. While there are Marxists in the revolution, there is no religious persecution here. If the Bishops Conference were made up of people who were more open-minded, perhaps the problems would not be stirred up, and the situation of the church would improve. Given their mind-sets, of course there are clashes, and they're going to continue. But the fact that there are Marxists in the government doesn't mean anything. They can coexist peacefully and constructively in a country where most people are Christians.

—*Each of three times the Nicaraguan government has sent an official delegation to the Vatican, seeking dialogue in the context of conflict and tension with the bishops of Nicaragua, you have been part of the delegation. What is your impression on the basis of those direct contacts with the Vatican?*

—Nicaragua has made a great effort, sending delegations to the Vatican three times, to give a better picture of the situation and in particular the government's relations with the hierarchy. There are few cases in history where a government has sent a delegation to the Vatican seeking good relations. We have always been made welcome in Rome, especially by Cardinal Casaroli. But in Rome there are different tendencies, just as everywhere else. As far as I'm concerned, Cardinal Casaroli understands the issues in Nicaragua very well. I'd go so far as to say that the cardinal understands the situation in Nicaragua better than some bishops in Nicaragua. He is very capable and has always tried to find a solution for Nicaragua's problems. In the case of the priests in the government he found an acceptable formula that has been working for some time now. But you realize that in a revolution there are new developments every day; new developments keep occurring and you have to keep solving problems because things don't stand still.

> **I have learned that in a storm you have to keep calm until the sun comes out.**

—To be president of the Supreme Court in a revolution, and especially in this Nicaraguan revolution, which broke with the whole juridical order and with class frameworks and structures, is difficult and uncomfortable. You have to keep your balance and only strength of character, faith, and an ideological awareness that Nicaragua has to change can keep you going. I have come to understand that you can't calm the storm nor the wild waves by means of the rudder in your hand; you have to keep calm until the sun comes out.

This position (in which I am serving simply out of idealism, since it does not benefit me economically) has brought me joy, bitterness and sadness, misunderstanding and criticism, praise and recognition, enthusiasm and disappointment. Even some of our relatives and family friends no longer come to see us. Others have criticized me sharply and I have felt hatred from people whose lives are full of venom. One of them, still very dear to me, went so far as to insult me at my daughter's wedding because I am identified with the Sandinista people's revolution. Not all have been hurt materially by the revolution. I never thought that my own stand with the revolution and the fact that it has hit others economically would affect our love and feelings as a family. Poor misguided people—I forgive them. Some day they will come to understand, whatever may happen, that my position is the right one to take vis-à-vis history and the generations to come, even though imperialism may try to destabilize our revolution. Public office comes and goes. If I am in this office it is not as an instrument, or because I am "being used," but rather out of conviction and faith in this revolution and what it wants to do.

I have had to bear all sorts of things and get used to it. My conscience is at rest and gives me strength to go ahead. I recognize that there are errors and failures at this critical period in the history of my people, a period of transition toward a new world, a road full of obstacles, but one that will lead us to a socialism suitable for our concrete reality in Nicaragua. That is my belief and my testimony.

Some time later I pass by Argüello's office in the Plaza España complex to pick up his curriculum vitae. I go up the steps, knock on the door, and then step into another environment: a room with dark wood, a red rug, and long white curtains.

He gives me a photocopy of his uncle Pedro Hurtado's pamphlet "Torture as a System." An impressive indictment of the Somoza regime, with a detailed description of Hurtado's arrest by Somoza agents on November 27, 1940, and of the barbaric torture he underwent in the dungeons of terror to force him to make false accusations against one of the dictator's political adversaries.

2

EMILIO E. BALTODANO

Comptroller General

"I am going to die as a member of the Catholic Church and as a revolutionary"

Emilio Enrique Baltodano was born in Diriamba on January 20, 1916. After graduating from a college run by the La Salle Brothers in Philadelphia in 1939, until 1976 he worked in Nicaragua on his family's lands and businesses: growing and processing coffee, rice, and other products, exporting coffee,

9

cotton, and sesame seed, and importing light agricultural equipment. In 1977 he left his businesses and lands in order to devote himself to anti-Somoza activity alongside the Sandinista National Liberation Front. As a member of the Twelve he alternated between political activity and exile. After the Sandinista victory in 1979, he was made Comptroller General of the Republic. He has been married to Gloria Antonia Cantarero since 1946, and their seven children, all married, work with the revolution in different ways.

●

Emilio Baltodano is a traditional, pious Catholic, 67 years old, concerned about church matters; he is likewise a convinced Sandinista revolutionary. The office in his house is small and bare. A table, his armchair, a bookstand, and two metal filing cabinets. "This spot is historic because of the clandestine meetings we held here," Don Emilio tells me with emotion. His day at the office is over. He is visibly tired and now I am going to subject him to extra effort.

"Our whole family joined the Sandinista Front during the revolution. We are all still alive—and all very united." Don Emilio says this with emotion in his large, tired eyes. I see them, with large pink eyelids, magnified through his thick glasses. I find this moving, since the revolution cost 50,000 Nicaraguan lives, and I have seen the survivors divided in many families. "Sometimes it frightens me," Don Emilio adds in a low voice.

●

Q—How many children do you have, Don Emilio?

Baltodano—Seven children and fifteen grandchildren. The fifteenth was just born the other day. All my children are involved in the revolution. Emilio as Minister of Industry, Alvaro in the Sandinista Army, Gerardo, Francisco, all of them in the revolution. And my daughters and sons-in-law also.

He speaks with the delight of an old tree trunk that is reborn in its branches and new shoots. "They are the best contribution I've made."

—Sixty-seven is an age for retirement. Why are you still working?

—I'm working for the revolution, for the people. In my post as Comptroller of the Republic I try to do my best for the state, for the people. A tricky job, yes? Difficult. In practice, it is impossible to accomplish all we want to do right away. We're getting everything ready in Nicaragua so there will be more control over things, so that what belongs to the people will be controlled and the corruption we inherited from forty some years of the Somoza regime will be gone forever. God willing before too long we'll get there, although I think it will take a few years.

—Why?

—Now it is hard, not because we have to weed out corrupt people (there aren't any, thank God), but because those who are working in the government are inexperienced in managing state property. We're learning. Besides, it will take years to change many people's mentality. I believe the idea of honest is somewhat relative: in Somoza's time, in a very corrupt environment, an average thief was honored, and a petty thief was considered a saint. Why? Because everything is in comparative terms. And we have to keep going to change the attitude of many Nicaraguans, especially people who did not have the privilege of getting a good education and who were inevitably deeply influenced by the customs of the Somoza period. At that time they often had to degrade themselves and adjust in order to make a living and support their family. They didn't get good salaries but politicians gave them things. And if they didn't cooperate, if they didn't close their eyes to certain things, they often couldn't eat.

—*Are you a Christian, Don Emilio?*

—I am a Christian. A Catholic. I have always been, I still am, and I will remain a Catholic.

—*How do you live your faith now? How do you practice your Christianity within the revolutionary process?*

—We've come out of an older world, where we blindly believed what our elders told us. For us, what they said was law. Then we began to open our eyes and to doubt whether this kind of Catholicism, this kind of Christianity, was best. Is this really what the Lord wants of us? we asked. We discovered great social injustices. We would see people who were considered saints but who were not saints at all when we saw them close up. We sometimes saw ourselves as good Catholics, with our communions, our Masses, our daily rosary. But was that what being a good Catholic, a good Christian, was all about?

I now know that a person shouldn't be praised just for those things. You don't go to Mass and take part in the Eucharist because you're a saint. No, you take part in the Eucharist because you need it, because you feel weak and sinful and you go for strength. Perhaps those of us who go to the Eucharist more, or in our family pray the rosary, do so because we feel we aren't as good as others, and we go for help. Especially now, with these responsibilities, in a new government where we feel subject to criticism. And people like me, old but inexperienced in this kind of work, we feel very weak and we know that if God doesn't help us we may fail. We need this help, especially in a government like ours, where there are different kinds of people all mixed together.

But I should tell you that despite the diversity there is something common to all of us who have responsibility in this revolutionary government, something very important, and that is a desire to end social injustice and to benefit the poor. We all share one conviction: happiness lies not in what you have in material goods but in what you are giving to others. That's why I don't look on the way I used to live as real Christianity, though I now feel I need God more than before, in order to keep up my strength and carry out my responsibility.

—*Besides what you give, your dedication, your work, which is a lot for your age, do you keep up any practices of the church?*

—Yes. First, the Eucharist. I go to the Eucharist. It's something I need, a food God gives me, the life of Christ.

Second, I make it a practice to see in every person a human being, a Christ, and to try to put myself in their place and feel things from their standpoint. I have to deal with many people and I have a great deal of responsibility. To some extent I do have authority but I am frightened at the thought of exercising it. Having such authority makes me afraid because I work with people whom I did not know well before, and I see the attitudes of many people here in Nicaragua and the way they manage state property, the people's property. I have to point out how they act. And I observe faults. Most of the faults we have seen come from inexperience. But from time to time you see faults due to bad will. Still, you are afraid to be very harsh, even though you feel you should. Why? Because you should put yourself in the situation of the other person, and examine, analyze, whether that person received an education like your own, from Christian teachers. And that is very hard, since at the same time you tell yourself: "It is up to me to determine whether this is going to continue or going to end, improving the situation." So then, something in your conscience makes you feel uncomfortable, it's something like being tired.

—*When did you become a Sandinista revolutionary, and why?*

—I became a revolutionary and a Sandinista when I was almost 60 years old—and that was because of what my children taught me.

—*How did that happen?*

—It had to do with my being a Christian. You see one day, one of my sons, right here in this room, asked me a question: "*Papa*, you've always preached Christianity, you've told us about the injustice going on, that it's enormous, that something has to be done. But in practice, what are you doing?" The son who asked me that was going to join the Sandinista Front. He wanted me to tell him, "OK, go on and join." But when he said that to me, I answered, "Son, you're not going to join by yourself; we're all going to join." And that's how it began.

—*Tell me about the Christian education you received during your childhood.*

—I was educated by Jesuits at the Colegio Centroamérica in Granada. That is where I got my Christian education. As a child, being with Christ was always something I felt in my heart. One thing the Jesuits taught me has stayed with me: love for neighbor. Conscience. Being conscientious about not deceiving anyone. You should be honest, because there is a God who, sooner or later, will reveal you and make you see what you are. During my school days I belonged to the Sodality of Mary and I was an altar boy. When I finished high school I went to the United States. That was 1934.

I went there with the idea of becoming a doctor but then I changed to business administration. I spent five years in the United States. When I came back to Nicaragua, I began to work with my brothers in businesses like coffee, planting rice, and so forth. I was twenty-three. Then in 1946 Gloria Antonia Cantarero and I were married, one October morning in the chapel of the archbishop of Managua.

When I got married I began to look at life more seriously. After a year our first daughter arrived. I think that's when I began to make a contribution to our country, by bringing up our children. Little by little. Anyway, the kind of Christianity I was living was very useful because that is what I preached to my children, although now I feel it was perhaps a bit deceptive and incomplete. The times we were living in were corrupt. I got married in 1946, you see, and Somoza was already in power. It was a corrupt period. True, I used to examine my conscience at that time and I told myself, "OK, I haven't robbed anybody, I'm not bribing anyone, I'm not involved in the Somoza system." But it did not occur to me that I was committing a tremendous sin, the sin of omission, of indifference. The situation of Nicaragua looked immoral to me at the time, because of the way *Somocismo* misused state property, because of the exploitation and because the people of Nicaragua were denied schools.

Religious life looked superstitious to me. Huge processions for the feast of St. Sebastian in Diriamba—they still exist. But deep down what did they have to do with real religion, with real knowledge of Christ and union with him? They are holiday celebrations, full of joy. For some people, business, for others, rest, a break in their work, dancing, having a few drinks, gambling. And even though this is all fine up to a point, I saw that when it came to real religion, to really thinking about God deep down in your own personal life, to what it means to have been created in God's image and likeness, to the fact that the way we will live in the future will depend on how we have acted, according to what we have contributed to the society we live in, I found that there was very little of that, of real faith commitment.

I was always telling my children these things, and I sent them to Catholic school, with the Christian Brothers and with the Calasanz Fathers, and they all finished with the Jesuits, for whom I feel a great deal of affection. That was my greatest contribution, because my children have become better Christians than I am. These children of mine have taught me with their example. They arrived at the point where they could disregard the material things I had, and they came to tell me that what they saw as worthwhile was the moral wealth I had given them. So on the basis of the Christian morality I had taught them, they decided to make the break to self-sacrifice and commitment to justice, to step over into the revolutionary struggle and to change the corrupt situation in the country. I always preached the most traditional Christian morality. But that was all they needed to take up the struggle against injustice. And so my son challenged me when he was going to join the Sandinista Front. He gave me my most valuable lesson.

> **I gave up my work, making money, and devoted myself to revolutionary work.**

—About three days after this talk with my son, I began selling things, selling property. And I gave up my work, making money, and devoted myself to revolutionary work. Later on, that same son was in Mexico and I often went to see him. It was there that the idea of setting up a Human Rights Commission in Nicaragua got its start, and I was able to move around as its secretary without arousing suspicion.

My work with the Front went in the direction of getting people like me, from my social sector, to become involved. On my trips to Mexico I got to know some Sandinistas who were working there on committees, and I always argued with them that in the bourgeois class, as they put it, some of us were not so bad and that we could come to an understanding with them and work with them. So after some time, someone from outside the country came to Nicaragua and sent a message saying he wanted to speak with me confidentially. We agreed to meet in a church, at Mass. I got there and found him and greeted him as though we hadn't seen each other for a long time and offered to take him home in my car. He said the leadership of the Sandinista Front wanted to have a meeting in Costa Rica and hoped I could host it. They wanted me to rent an apartment under my name. I was to go there and live in it for a few days, and then some friends would arrive. They didn't tell me who.

I agreed and went to Costa Rica, supposedly on business. I rented the apartment and one day a group of fourteen or fifteen arrived. Some of them belonged to the Directorate of the Sandinista Front. Commander Humberto Ortega was there. He explained the situation of the Front and proposed that we join them and that we tell him who else among our class might take part. We were there for three days and we all took on the commitment. We agreed to try to recruit people. Nevertheless, none of us dared to recruit a soul. I think that was good. That meeting was so confidential that we all took it very seriously, and we kept it a secret. We were afraid to tell others to become involved, and we only spoke with those who, even if they were not at the meeting, were already on the list that the *compañeros* in the Front had drawn up.

Don Emilio has had coffee brought in and offers me some. As he tells his story he takes small sips of black coffee from a large mug.

—Out of that came the formation of the famous group called the Twelve. Later, we had a week-long meeting in Mexico out on a country place. José Benito Escobar and other Sandinista members were there. We laid out almost the whole plan for a new government. We planned the cabinet, and I think 80 percent of the people we selected came into the government after victory. There were other meetings, other rendezvous, some here, others in Costa Rica. Then at one point it was decided that we were going to strike and we learned what the password would be. When we got it, we would have five days to get to Costa Rica. One day, as I was coming out of Mass with my wife, someone I didn't know came up and gave the password. My wife didn't know anything about it.

We got together in Costa Rica. On October 14, 1977, in the wee hours of the morning we were going to come across the southern border with *muchachos* of the Sandinista Front and take Nicaragua. But the plan didn't work because things weren't really ready and coordination broke down. There wasn't any uprising in the middle of the country. There was a strong attack in San Carlos, Cardenas, and another strike in the north, but the effort in the center of the country broke down. We went back to San José very discouraged. We spent a whole day discussing things. Morale was very low. But after that whole day we came to the conclusion that we should openly declare war on Somoza. And we all decided to commit ourselves. So we worked out the first communiqué of the Twelve, signed by all of us there. With that piece of paper we called on the whole population to work with the Sandinista Front, and we tried to make people see that it was the Sandinista Front that had been giving its own life and blood to liberate Nicaragua.

> **I saw that the Sandinistas were more Christian than many of us who went to Mass every Sunday.**

After releasing that communiqué with our signatures we had no alternative but to become involved in the anti-Somoza struggle one hundred percent. We were now completely committed. We thought it was very necessary to get international relations going and to get international help. We particularly had in mind some important governments, and we wanted their help in changing the image of the Sandinista Front, since many figured that if they were guerrillas they must be thieves and bandits. We saw that this was clearly not true.

—*Actually, how were they, Don Emilio? How did you find the Sandinistas?*

—As I got to know them closely, I began to see them as more Christian than I was, more Christian than many people who go to Mass every Sunday. They were so utterly unconcerned about themselves, and so concerned about saving the country, and helping the poor with no interest in what they would get out of it. For me, that explains how the war of liberation was so successful. Somoza's National Guard was strong but the Guard measured what it gave with the pay it got. A Sandinista only gave, only wanted to give, and to give more than anything else. In other words, the Sandinista gave of himself or herself.

—*What did the group of the Twelve do when you came back to Nicaragua in July 1978, challenging Somoza?*

—I find it surprising that Somoza didn't kill us during those six months we were here, from July to January. Why did he make such a mistake? We spent our time stirring up the population to rise against Somoza. We asked the Guard to disregard its head. We went all over the nine provinces every weekend. And during the week we spent our time making press statements and getting ready for the weekend. Wherever we went, we got enthusiastic receptions. In Estelí, León, Jinotega, Ocotal, Boaco, and in small towns. We came to see that 80 or 90 percent of the people were with us. Then came the spectacular occupation of the National Palace and the attacks on León and Chinandega. At that point we suspended demonstrations because it was practically impossible to hold them.

After what happened in León and Chinandega, with so much killing that we were all living in terror, the United States offered to mediate. We were involved in that. We had representatives there with the aim of not giving in, of remaining independent. Whenever anyone asked, as U.S. government people used to do, we answered, "We asked only one thing of you, that you stay out; leave us alone, don't get involved in our war." Finally we broke with the mediation. We put out a strong communiqué, saying that to continue the process would be to sell out our country, and that what the gringos were doing was not mediation but intervention.

At that point we took asylum in the Mexican Embassy; we thought we had gone as far as we could. We were there a month and a half, but we continued our political activities. When it became known that those who were involved in "mediation" meetings were working out an agenda for a week of discussions that would end in a pact,* we were worried and decided to leave the embassy. There had been an amnesty. We all went to our homes one Sunday night. On Monday we held a press conference and strongly criticized those who were involved in the mediation. The United States ambassador was so nervous that he called a halt to the whole program he had set up, prepared a document of agreement, and gave the Somocistas and the opposition forty-eight hours to sign it. This document asked for a peacekeeping force for Nicaragua—in other words, intervention. The opposition signed it. These opposition people, who are always in opposition (the same ones who are in opposition today, and logically so, since then they were asking for intervention!)—these people did not measure up. To top it off Somoza came out on TV and insulted them, told them he was a patriot, and out of patriotism would not sign. For us, that was a victory. In a way, Somoza broke with the gringos.†

---

*In Nicaragua the word "pact" had a particular significance, referring to deals Somoza made with the political opposition.—TRANS.

†The Sandinista occupation of the National Palace and the uprisings in several Nicaraguan cities so alarmed the U.S. government that it began to seek a negotiated settlement, which many feared would be equivalent to *Somocismo* without Somoza. The Broad National Front (FAO), led by businessman Alfonso Robelo, continued negotiations after the Twelve withdrew, only to be rejected by Somoza. In early 1979 the FAO realigned itself with the Sandinistas, and Robelo was part of the first junta. He resigned in April 1980 and eventually left the country to head ARDE, the political faction of the contras allied with Eden Pastora.—TRANS.

We had no choice but to leave the country again and to continue the struggle from outside. One by one we left. They didn't give us visas, but we took advantage of the corruption of the Somoza system, and by paying two or three thousand pesos apiece, we got them. We went to Mexico and Venezuela. Reinaldo Tefel and I had to go to the Dominican Republic and Puerto Rico. We continued to seek international aid and to explain to people in other countries the exploitation our country was suffering. Finally, the moment came: Somoza was tottering. There were international pressures, confidential discussions, and the final offensive. The Somoza machine was defeated, and the new government came in on July 19, 1979.

—During this whole period of struggle against Somoza, what role did the Christian faith play for you?

—When we went to other countries, they asked us, "Why are people like you allied with the Sandinista Front? What impels you to do this? That question was put to me and I answered, "Our Christian principles." For me it was clear that that was what motivated me. I wanted to make reparation for my earlier sin of omission. That is what impelled me to join the Sandinista Front. And on different occasions, I said to Carlos Andrés Pérez, former president of Venezuela, and to Aristides Royo, the president of Panama, "When you talk about these Sandinistas, do you know who they are? I have a list of the *muchachos* and one of them is a son of mine. Another is a son of Dr. Joaquín Cuadra Chamorro, and others are from the Carrión and the Lang families, many of them professional people who have graduated from the Jesuit university in Managua and other universities. They are Christians, and they are up in the mountains carrying rifles. They are not murderers or bandits, as some people say." And that made a great impression. The great fear people had of helping Nicaragua melted away.

Capitalists in Nicaragua and other countries accuse everyone of being communist. They want to take the word "Christian" away from us in order to smear the revolution, to eliminate aid, and to isolate us. But it was precisely my Christian faith that moved me into this struggle and keeps me there. If I didn't have Christian faith—why, instead of joining the Front, with all the sacrifice and renunciation it has cost me, I would be taking things safe and easy.

—Has your Christianity changed in this revolutionary struggle? What tensions, breaks, or conflicts have you experienced?

—Sometimes I feel a bit nervous about my present Christianity, because it is no longer just what was taught me and inculcated in me when I was a child. I've often felt fear sweeping over me, and I've had to think things through again. I've looked for people to talk with, good priests who could clear up some scruples I've had because I'm no longer the conventional Christian I learned to be. The tradition and customs you take on as a child obviously influence you a great deal, even though your new convictions are sharp and firm. The first Christian principles I received are still in me. They have not been denied, but they have been broadened and have grown.

During a retreat, I overcame my scruples about violence.

—There's something else I want to tell you. When we were about to go to Costa Rica, when we had given money and were willing to give more and to help the struggle, a thought came to me, challenging me. I heard Archbishop Obando and some priests speaking about bloodshed and violence. They said it had to be avoided, so I had strong scruples. I spoke to one priest, a friend of mine, and managed to go away to a house to make a week-long retreat. I came out of that retreat with spiritual courage and no more scruples. I was convinced that if there was going to be bloodshed, bloodshed that would bring us all enormous suffering, we were at least going to stop the ongoing bloodshed of all the poor and humble people, blood that we didn't see flowing, but that had been flowing for many years. We were going to bring about what Christ said: the poor are moving up and the rich are moving down. So I got rid of my scruples.

About two weeks after I made this retreat we made our trip to Costa Rica. I felt enthusiastic even though we were hearing news of many people killed. That was painful. Often that gave you the shivers. But we saw that as something that simply had to happen, as painful as it was. And you said to yourself, "Maybe I should be there." But at my age I couldn't go. I couldn't give what my children were giving. My children were there. One of my sons was among those who attacked Masaya in 1977, "the suicide attack" as they called it. I was following the news from Costa Rica. Radio stations were directly connected with those in Nicaragua. You could hear shots, ambulances, and someone say, "So many have been killed, so many Sandinistas have been killed." I knew my son was one of the commanders there. I didn't sleep that night, but I accepted this as something that was unavoidable and necessary for the good of the whole people, and I lived through that with my Christian faith. Two or three days later, I got word that my son was alive.

—*Don Emilio, what do you think of the positions other Christians and part of the hierarchy have taken against the revolutionary process?*

—That is one of the problems that I regard as most serious and most troublesome, as a Christian and as a Sandinista. We are going through the breaking of relations between a sector of the church and our government. Notice that I do not say "the church" but "a sector of the church." That is because we are all the church and there are many of us Christians who are not breaking with the government. But it is sad to see that some people, especially in our hierarchy, do not understand this change, and allow themselves to be influenced and to be used. Why is that? I don't know. But you have seen that people have often sought dialogue with the archbishop and he has refused. I myself was in a meeting in his house once with a small group, speaking about dialogue. And the archbishop—I say this with all respect—closed the door on us. He spoke about the church's legal order and what the authority of the bishops is, things that no one understands today, things that I think no longer exist in practice, even if they are written in some law codes somewhere. This kind of authoritarianism no longer exists in practice and no one understands it anymore. And then the kind of scruples I was mentioning hit me again.

Don Emilio laughs, with both simplicity and astuteness.

—*Don Emilio, those of you who are Christian and are taking part in this process are accused of collaborating with totalitarianism and of leading Nicaragua to atheism.*

—Look, I don't think there's anyone in the world who is a hundred percent good or a hundred percent bad. This government is now under a magnifying glass. If someone wants to magnify the mistakes we make (it would be stupid to say we don't make them) and wants to overlook the good things we do, well that's a matter for that person's conscience. Now, when what they say is serious and has serious consequences, and the people who say it and magnify it and spread it are people with a high educational level, and when they don't see the good and only look at the defects and magnify them, I'm afraid they're doing that out of bad faith and to protect their own interests.

I sincerely believe that our defects, mistakes, and imperfections are small; we are not doing the horrible things some accuse us of. I think what they ought to do, if they have good will, is join the process and correct what is bad and improve what is good—I mean from within, because it can't be done from outside. When someone tells me, "You people shouldn't be there because this government is not Christian," and so forth, I answer, "All the more reason why I should be inside the government, just because I am a Christian. I want to sow the seed of Christianity inside." That is what I tell my friends and my children. That is what they taught us in the church a long time ago; we have to take our Christianity everywhere and put it where it doesn't exist, in all kinds of situations.

I am going to die as a Christian and a revolutionary, but I'm horrified to think that my children might go on as revolutionaries and not as Christians.

—*Don Emilio, how do you view the future of the revolution and the future of Christianity in Nicaragua, given the many problems, the harassment, threats, aggressions, divisions. . . ?*

—Despite how serious and worrisome all that is, I have hope in the revolution, because we have these young people of ours. But we have to make sacrifices. We can't leave it all up to young people. Older people must make a great effort. The period in history we are living through demands that we Christians give our all.

I have the impression that Christianity has deteriorated among our young people, that their religious spirit has been put to sleep. You see little interest in basic aspects of Christianity, such as having a life of prayer and of Eucharist. I believe that one factor that contributes a lot to this is the way church people have criticized the revolution. Young people are seeing the church in a ridiculous situation, in an unjust position, when they see it oppose the people's process, and so they stop believing in the church. So some priests and bishops are doing horrifying damage to the church. They are criticizing something that, taken as a whole, the young people think is just, and good, and indispensable for Nicaragua.

That is how they experience it, often making great sacrifices so the process can go ahead. And these young people say, "How can it be un-Christian, how can it be unjust and wrong for me, with my rich parents, to go away from home, up to the mountains, to be a soldier, sleep in a tiny house, sometimes even a hut, and sacrifice myself for the good of the whole people? And this bishop tells me that I'm unjust, that I'm anti-Christian, and that I'm fomenting hatred." For young people that is very serious, because for them the bishop represents the church. They don't have the idea that we are all the church. And so they feel as though they're outside, chased out, thrown out of the church.

Those of us who are Christians of a certain age and have received a certain kind of formation, have come together in communities of "Christians in the Revolution," and we have an awareness of being church and a desire to be church and to manifest it publicly. I hope we always remain as church. I have no idea if it could happen that the bishops could come along and excommunicate us. Well, you have to be ready.

Don Emilio laughs heartily this time.

—I'm not going to feel excommunicated. Years ago that would have terrified me. Now if they do it—I say this in all sincerity—I would not feel excommunicated. And when I found a priest who would give me communion, I would receive it. My sons can see this. You can have scruples, have your doubts, but you have to act, and to come up with solutions. In that spirit, relying on God, who cannot abandon us, I am hopeful about the future of Christianity in Nicaragua.

I want to tell you what I told Bishop Barni, who was bishop of Matagalpa before and is now bishop of León, in a meeting our Christian group had with him. I said, "I'm going to die a Christian and a revolutionary, but I am horrified to think that my children might go on as revolutionaries but not as Christians because the church itself chased them out."

A few days after the interview Don Emilio became very sick. He came close to death and remained so for several weeks. I remembered his concern and his hope, his firm will to die as a member of the Catholic Church and as a revolutionary. After a difficult but successful operation, Don Emilio recovered and has gone back to work.

3

CARLOS TÜNNERMANN

Minister of Education

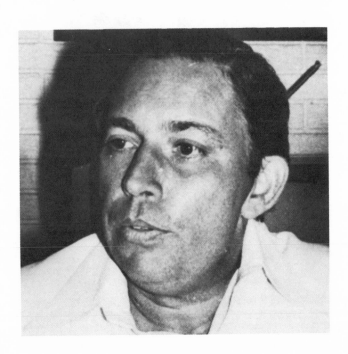

"I joined the Sandinista revolution through a Christian decision"

Born in Managua in 1933, Carlos Tünnermann studied law at the National University of Nicaragua. Because of the corruption of the justice system under Somoza, he chose to become a law professor at the National University instead of practicing law. He was elected rector in 1964 and was twice reelected, holding the position until 1974. He has been General Secretary of the Confed-

eration of Central American Universities (CSUCA) (1959-1964), President of the Union of Universities of Latin America (UDUAL) (1969-70 and 1972-74), and on the board of directors of the International Association of Universities (1970-75). In 1975 he was made director of UNESCO's programs in Colombia and from 1977 to 1979 he was director of CSUCA's Program for Scientific and Technological Development. He was one of the group known as the Twelve. In 1979 he became Minister of Education in the revolutionary government. In 1984 he was made the Nicaraguan ambassador in Washington. He is married to Rosa Carlota Pereira and they have seven children. Among his works are La Universidad: búsqueda permanente *(León, 1971);* La Educación Superior de Colombia *(Bogotá, 1978);* De la Universidad y su problemática *(Mexico, 1980);* Hacia una nueva educación en Nicaragua *(León, 1980);* Ensayos sobre la universidad latinoamericana y estudios sobre la teoría de la universidad *(San José, Costa Rica, 1981).*

●

His office as minister looks like a salon. There are areas for working at a desk, for carrying on a conversation in comfortable armchairs, for classifying papers, publications, materials. The floor is carpeted and there are many pictures on the walls: portraits of Rubén Darío, José Martí, Germán Pomares, Sandino, Carlos Fonseca, a large photo of participants in the literacy program, flags of Nicaragua and the Sandinista Front.

On time, alert, serious, concerned about details, cultured, and precise (his imperturbability is a surprise in this part of the world), Education Minister Tünnermann sits at his desk.

●

Tünnermann—My participation in the people's revolution as a militant in the Sandinista Front and as Minister of Education in the Government of National Reconstruction is something I do as a Christian. I live my life from the perspective of my Christian faith.

We've put our priority on the educational needs of those sectors of the population who have been most left out and left behind.

Q—The Ministry of Education is a key post in a revolution like this. Obviously, cultural revolution is the most urgent need at the heart of every revolution. What has your ministry done?

—There's no doubt that the task of educating the people is a priority task in a revolution. Education is now being provided as something to which people have a right. In the past that right to education wasn't recognized. If we compare the situation in the Somoza period with what we have done since the revolutionary victory, it's clear that we have put a priority on the educational needs of those sectors that were most left out and left behind—starting with illiterate peasants.

Just one month after the victory we assumed the task of organizing and coordinating the National Literacy Crusade. In fact even before the victory, when we were still in San José (Costa Rica), the first task the FSLN set me was to prepare an outline or a sketch of plans for teaching the people to read and write on a large scale. This was in order to fulfill a point that had historically always been a part of Sandinista programs. That was true even back in the time of General Augusto César Sandino, who encouraged his guerrilla fighters to learn to read and write and gave them a chance to do so. Carlos Fonseca also used to emphasize the need for literacy in all his manifestos.

The most important thing we've done so far in the field of education is to teach reading and writing. We have thus brought a basic minimum of education to peasants and others whom no one had taught to read and write in the past. It was better for the system in power to keep the peasants and the poor classes of the country in ignorance so they could more easily be manipulated and exploited. Hence we encountered a tremendous level of illiteracy: 50.3 percent of the population over ten years of age. That was the national average. In some provinces, especially in rural areas, it was as high as 85 percent. The literacy campaign enabled us to bring reading, writing, and the basic elements of mathematics to the peasant masses and to workers in cities and small communities. This has undoubtedly been the first great program of the Sandinista people's revolution.

We provide free education for everyone and we subsidize church schools without interfering in the teaching of religion.

The second contribution is the free education provided by the state. Previously the state didn't take care of the pre-school level; the nursery schools were all private. Of the nine thousand children receiving pre-school education in the past, fewer than a thousand were in classrooms connected to state grammar schools. Now, however, we have more than thirty-five thousand children in pre-school programs, and they're free. We've set these pre-schools up in poor barrios, alongside the big market areas, and in rural communities where poor children didn't have the slightest chance of any pre-school attention.

Grammar school is completely free, of course. In the past, high school was theoretically free, but in practice it wasn't, since the state institutes charged a monthly fee, varying from 20 to 40 córdobas, which they called a "voluntary contribution" for maintenance expenses and for buying materials. Because of this monthly charge, many young people couldn't go to high school. A decree was passed in the first few days after the revolutionary victory that schooling would be really free at all levels, including higher education, where now the only charges are for the student identity card and the fee for joining the National Students Union (less than 100 córdobas a semester). So because education is really free, more children and young people can go to school. This promotes equality of opportunity. So that's another great accomplishment.

By means of special agreements with about twenty-five private schools, mostly Catholic, we've been able to make these schools free, coeducational, and public, since the state has assumed the responsibility for paying teachers' salaries and administrative expenses. We've signed this kind of agreement with many religious congregations. Now these schools have opened their enrollment to other social classes. They're no longer for the elites of the country, but they serve children and young people from all social strata.

Basic to these agreements is the understanding that the state's economic role does not limit the Christian orientation these schools provide in their programs of religious education. I think these agreements also open up a new perspective for the work of schools run by religious congregations, especially schools in poor barrios, where tuition is out of the question.

Another important thing that's been done in the field of education is to diversify middle education, putting priority on technical/industrial education, agricultural education, and all forms of vocational education. This means introducing the idea that all education should be connected to work and avoiding the idea that education is a way of escaping from manual work. On the contrary, education should be a combination of manual and intellectual work, of theory and practice, of classroom and shopfloor. So far our experiments with work/school have been rather unsystematic, but we have put the students in contact with manual work. Some of those efforts, such as Basic Production Cycles, Rural Schools of Education/Work, and Agricultural Schools for Small Farmers, are systematically connected with productive work. In these programs the students get the moral education that is part of primary and secondary teaching in the Basic Cycle, and at the same time they take part in productive tasks in the fields. They take up projects in raising rabbits, in gardening, raising poultry, and so on, and these projects sometimes produce enough to supply food for the school lunch program and even to sell. For the future our idea is to connect rural schools to production centers so the student will be more involved in work and will contribute to the tasks of production.

It would take a long time to recount all the achievements we consider relevant. For example, in Nicaragua, for the first time in Latin America, before defining the ends and objectives of what the new education should be, we thought it would be a good idea to consult with the people in their organizations. A National Consultation on the Ends and Objectives of Education was set up. By means of a questionnaire, with fifty-five questions covering the whole gamut of educational problems, some thirty organizations in the country were consulted, including labor unions, student organizations, universities, teachers organizations, the Conference of Religious, the Bishops Conference, the National Association of the Clergy, the Chamber of Commerce, the Chamber of Industries, political parties, the army, the police—in a word, all the key organizations in the life of the country.

There was a broad response. Some institutions in the private sector and some political parties refused to participate in the consultation, perhaps because they thought we wouldn't make use of the responses. The fact is that we have used them. They were studied systematically and, on that basis, a proposal for ends or objectives of the new education was outlined. It is now being discussed thoroughly in weekly working meetings of the National Advisory Council on Education. Teachers, students, parents, the Conference of Religious, the National Federation of Catholic Schools, the Ministry of Planning, the Sandinista Central Federation of Workers, the Association of Rural Workers, and others all participate in the Council. This will guarantee that when we lay out our definition of ends and objectives, it will be the result of broad participation and so it will reflect what the Nicaraguan people think about what the new education should be. That education should promote the values we are striving for, values that will be embodied in plans and curricula, so as to form the new person.

—*Have you always been involved in education? What did you study, and what else have you done professionally?*

—I went to grammar school and high school with the Christian Brothers at the Pedagogical Institute for Boys in Managua. Then I studied in the National University of Nicaragua at the law school in León. I was there for five years. When I was getting ready for my final examinations in order to graduate, the dictator Anastasio Somoza García was executed by Rigoberto López Pérez. One of my fellow students was involved in that action, in the sense that they accused him of "concealing" it, that is, that he had known of the plan to execute Somoza and had not told the authorities. He had to face a military court. That fellow student chose me as his defense lawyer. The military court accepted me, even though I hadn't graduated, but had simply finished my studies and I defended him. Of course he was found guilty, as was everyone else accused, since the military court from the start intended to find them all guilty. That fellow student is today a Commander of the revolution, *compañero* Tomás Borge Martínez.

> **Disillusioned by the corruption, I gave up my career as a lawyer in order to become a university professor.**

I was disillusioned by this experience with military justice; it was completely useless to try to prove that Tomás was innocent. I'm still convinced that Tomás didn't play any significant role there. Although people had told him something could happen, he never believed it could actually happen, that is, he didn't have any certain knowledge that there would be an assassination attempt. At that time people thought there was practically no chance of killing Somoza García, with all the military apparatus he always had around him. At that point I became very disillusioned about the possibility of working as a lawyer in Nicaragua, since laws weren't obeyed. I felt there was no point in striving to work responsibly as a lawyer.

Around that time, early 1957, Dr. Mariano Fiallos Gil was appointed rector of the National University. As a student I had been his teaching assistant and we had worked together on some proposals aimed at gaining university autonomy. Dr. Fiallos called me in and said he wanted to appoint me general secretary of the university, and so he asked me to hurry and finish my graduation examinations. The resistance of the president, Luis Somoza, had first to be overcome. The day after my graduation I was appointed general secretary of the university. We began to work on the proposal for gaining university autonomy* and it was won in March 1958. And so I completely switched careers, from being a lawyer to becoming a professor and university administrator. I worked as general secretary of the university for two years alongside Fiallos, the rector.

Then when CSUCA, the regional organization linking the universities of Central America, was restructured at a meeting held in León in May 1959, it was decided to appoint a permanent General Secretary to take care of the responsibilities involved with it. The Central American rectors appointed me to that position. So I moved to San José (Costa Rica) and lived there for almost five years in order to work with this organization. This work gave me a Central American perspective and enabled me to gain a deeper knowledge of the problems facing the whole region. The work was absorbing and important; the universities were a good example of Central American spirit. Even though the governments weren't really and sincerely behind an effective integration of our peoples, the universities felt a real Central American vocation and sought to integrate our countries in culture and education.

---

*"University autonomy" in Latin America legally protects a university from government intervention and forbids the police and army to come onto its grounds. This is a safeguard for freedom of inquiry and expression. In practice, universities can then become relatively safe areas for expressions of opposition. It is understandable that the Somoza dictatorship was slow to grant autonomy.

While I was in San José, the rector, Fiallos Gil, died, and university colleagues proposed my name as candidate for rector. I was elected in October 1964, in spite of a great deal of opposition on the part of Luis and Anastasio Somoza, who never forgave me for having defended Tomás Borge. Besides, to them I was always a "subversive," an "immature" youth, a Marxist-communist. I stayed on as rector of the university until March 1974. I spent ten years as rector, and had to battle to defend the autonomy of the university and to stand up to the aggressive attacks made by the governments of Luis Somoza [1957–1963] and Anastasio Somoza [1967–1979]. For a while things moved back to a certain calm during the time when René Schick [1963–1966] was president, since he showed a bit more understanding with regard to university autonomy. During the whole first period of Anastasio Somoza Debayle, attacks against the university intensified as did efforts to strangle it economically. Taking advantage of the government of Dr. René Schick and with a good deal of organizing and demonstrating, we managed to gain a constitutional guarantee that the university would be autonomous and that it would receive two percent of the national budget.

While I was rector the university kept up an ongoing critique of the system, and was publicly known for its continuing denunciation of abuses. In addition, my personal sympathy for all movements in opposition to Somoza was obvious. So Somoza found a way to let me know that when I finished my term as rector it would be "better for me to leave Nicaragua," since I would no longer enjoy the presumed "immunity" my position gave me.

I first went to the United States on a Guggenheim fellowship to prepare a series of studies on the university in Latin America, taking advantage of the wealth of materials in the Library of Congress in Washington. Immediately afterwards UNESCO appointed me director of its program in Colombia. I left the job in UNESCO when Sergio Ramírez invited me to take part in the activities of the group of the Twelve. I moved to San José (Costa Rica) in order to dedicate myself openly to political work. So my work has not been as a lawyer but rather as an educator or as an educational administrator. And in this field I'm self-taught, since I haven't taken systematic courses in education. But I've worked in education my whole life and I consider myself more an educator than a lawyer.

I always admired Sandino's heroic anti-imperialism and I personally witnessed Carlos Fonseca's generous and unassailable conduct.

—How did you discover Sandino and how did you come to appreciate Sandinismo *so much that you would commit yourself to it in your civic and political struggle on behalf of the people of Nicaragua?*

—From the time I was in high school, from my childhood, when it was practically forbidden to pronounce Sandino's name, and when I used to hear it said that Sandino had been a bandit, I wondered whether this might not be a big lie, and whether Sandino in fact might not have been our country's greatest hero. Through books I could get hold of as they were passed around secretly, I got to know different versions of Sandino's deeds, his struggle against imperialism and against intervention. I've always been deeply nationalistic without, I think, being chauvinistic. I do recognize the value of internationalism. That is, I reject every kind of intervention in our country, no matter where it comes from. So for me because one man made up his mind to confront the greatest power in the world with very slim resources, one man incarnated the dignity of our country during his own time, I believed that man to be a really extraordinary person. So my admiration for Sandino goes back to my childhood.

In the university I knew Carlos Fonseca and had personal contact with him for a period of time. I knew him well when he was a student. I always admired his character: he was ascetic, idealistic, intelligent, studious, and had suffered a lot. He lived in the *Casa del Estudiante* [Student House] where the poorest students in the university could live free. I was then, from 1957 to 1958, general secretary of the university. When university autonomy was to be inaugurated in June 1958, we agreed to have a solemn ceremony, and Fiallos, the rector, asked me to look for a student who could speak in the name of all the students on such a historic occasion. This would mark the first series of university courses in which the university would enjoy the autonomy that had been granted the previous March.

I thought Carlos Fonseca would be the most appropriate one to speak, so I looked him up, and in the name of the rector proposed that he take part in the ceremony. And he did it. He did it very respectfully, very well, explaining how university autonomy was coming to Nicaragua forty years late, which was the truth. It had been achieved in other countries around 1918 or 1920, but we were inaugurating autonomy in 1958, in other words, forty years late. Carlos Fonseca went on to say that Nicaragua was a half century behind because of the dictatorship. He gave a brilliant speech. While we were presiding over the ceremony, Dr. Fiallos commented to me, "People should keep their eyes on this young man. He's going to be a great leader!" Commander-in-chief of the revolution, no less! But Carlos Fonseca impressed me also as an honest person, one so committed that he couldn't be turned away from his ideals. He might be a convinced Marxist, as he was, but I believe he was also, in a way, a Christian—at least in his unassailable and generous personal behavior and in the values for which he was struggling, the same values that gave the impetus to the movement he founded, the Sandinista National Liberation Front. It was his inspired idea to connect the anti-Somoza struggle to Sandino's anti-imperialism.

So my personal acquaintance with Carlos Fonseca was joined to my admiration for Sandino. Admittedly, later on, when I was rector and Fonseca was the leader of the Sandinista National Liberation Front, there were times when we had different opinions on how the university should be run, in view of the harassment it was getting from the dictatorship. I remember well how he sometimes wrote Sandinista Front documents or flyers for the students in which he criticized the way I was acting as rector, since he expected the university to be more at the forefront of the struggle against the dictatorship.

I was always of the opinion that it was important to hold on to university autonomy and not risk intervention so that we could have freedom for teaching and for the kind of political movement that enabled us to develop consciousness among so many young people who then became involved in the struggle and joined the Sandinista Front. I thought we should always struggle against the dictatorship from the university on an institutional level, without directly committing it to armed struggle so Somoza wouldn't have any excuse for attacking us and abolishing autonomy. That would have pushed the country back both politically and culturally. I'm familiar with some documents in which Carlos criticized the university for not responding with the degree of commitment to the struggle he would have liked. But that didn't mean that I didn't understand how he, in the thick of the struggle, would have liked the university to be more involved. I had another idea on how the university should take part in that struggle.

But what I want to stress is that these two figures, Sandino and Carlos Fonseca, had a great influence on my joining with *Sandinismo* and the FSLN.

It was a process of Christian reflection that led me to decide to collaborate with the FSLN.

—*You're a Catholic. How do you profess your Christianity publicly now?*
—At present I profess it publicly by acknowledging the fact that I'm a Christian whenever it is necessary to do so, but I don't feel any need to make a display or show off the fact that I'm a Christian. In some instances, when the church hierarchy has taken certain positions and it has been necessary to state the government's position toward religion, I've expressed my opinions from the viewpoint of a Christian committed to the process.

I go to Mass on the weekend, Saturdays or Sundays, with my family. I don't hide the fact that I'm a Christian, a Catholic, from anyone. For me, there is absolutely no opposition between Christianity and *Sandinismo*. Nor does the fact that I'm a Christian pose any problem for my full involvement in the revolutionary process.

I belong to the group called Christians in the Revolution. That's a group of us who believe that we Christians should be committed to this revolutionary process because it embodies values that are, in fact, Christian, and it is working for the majority of the people in this country. In the process we're discovering and putting into practice the option for the poor, the preferential option that we should undertake as Christians. We take part in the process in different ways. Some of us are government employees and others are private citizens, professional people, or university professors. But all of us believe that as Christians we have a place in this revolution and we don't encounter any obstacle to our Christianity in the revolution. We believe there is a great convergence between what the revolutionary is striving for and what the Christian is striving for, and that many of the revolution's programs satisfy our Christian concern that the poor have their needs met more than government programs did in the past.

—*Does your Christian faith have any influence on your political involvement and your professional work in the revolution?*

—Yes. I think what I am doing is deeply rooted in Christianity. In fact, my decision to begin working with the Sandinista National Liberation Front came about through a process of Christian reflection. I thought to myself, "OK, what do we have in Nicaragua at this point? We have a bloodthirsty dictatorship; an oppressive system; a privileged class utterly oblivious of their brothers and sisters, the poor and the oppressed; a class that is satisfied to some extent, since Somoza guarantees them the peace and order they need for doing business. This privileged class of people, who claim to be Christian because they go to Mass, have their children baptized, have their daughters get married in church, and so forth, deep down they know—they're not unaware since they're educated people—that their businesses, their plantations, are based on a system that is corrupt and based on exploitation, a system that certainly has little of Christianity about it.

In view of this situation I asked myself—or rather we asked ourselves, since in the group of the Twelve there were priests like Father Miguel D'Escoto and Father Ernesto Cardenal—"What should a Christian do faced with such a regime? In this situation who is it that is really struggling to change and transform all this?" And so we recognized that those who were giving Christian witness were the *muchachos* of the Sandinista Front.

We recognized that in Nicaragua the possibility of embodying Christian values could only become a reality by means of a revolution, and that those who were working for such a revolution were the young people of the Sandinista Front. The traditional opposition political parties always came around to some accommodation with Somoza. We also recognized that members of the private business sector had begun to turn against Somoza. That happened after the 1972 earthquake, when Somoza moved into their areas of business and began to engage in unfair competition with them. It was only when their privileges and interests were affected that they changed toward Somoza. Obviously it was not out of Christian conviction, nor because they thought the country should be changed in order to carry out programs to serve the most needy classes. They did it because at that point their interests were clashing with Somoza's. That was when they came out in support of the idea that Somoza should leave office, believing that with some small reforms and superficial changes they could keep control of the situation and hold onto power in the country and in that way safeguard their longstanding privileges.

My personal decision to support the Sandinista National Liberation Front and to commit myself to its struggle took place because I became convinced that in order to change this situation Nicaragua had to go through an armed struggle, even though we didn't like the idea. Besides, out of plain honesty, we Christians had to recognize that the Sandinista Front was the only force that had a real chance of leading the country to a structural and social transformation that would make it possible for fundamental values of Christianity to become a reality.

I think the educational programs we're carrying out are deeply Christian.

—It is my feeling that in this work my Christian life is growing. I don't know whether it's the same in other areas, but in the field of education I find that there is enormous Christian achievement in all the programs we're carrying out. For example, on weekends, when I go to inaugurate schools in small rural communities in Nicaragua, I see the people happy, satisfied because they've made a classroom with their own hands. We gave them the materials and they provided the land and built the walls and roof of the classroom where their children will now go to school. When I feel the children's happiness, when they have a school for the first time and they see nicely made wooden desks where they can sit, then I feel a great deal of satisfaction, and that satisfaction is both revolutionary and Christian.

For example, last Saturday, in the community of El Contrabando, near El Tránsito beach, a woman said, "The politicians of the past used to come here with trucks on election day to pick us up and so we'd go to Managua to vote, and then they brought us back, and lots of people came back drunk or were left lying in the streets of Managua. They never remembered us again. We used to hear offers of schools and health centers and a lot of things that never came true. But now the things we've always heard about are becoming real. Here's the school, and now we're ready to start the health center next door, since we've learned how to build by doing the school. Then we're going to build a community center, and then our own houses, now that we've learned how." That was what that humble woman in that community said. This program of community schools teaches peasants the basic elements of carpentry, cement work, and construction, and that enables them to go ahead with their own programs. So when I look there and see the happy expression on the faces of children and the peasants now that they finally have their school, I think to myself, "Well, this is something that is deeply Christian."

When, in the National Literacy Crusade, I see the young people in the upper-class families of Managua, living alongside peasants under difficult conditions, and when I see in these young people, as I can see in my own, the affection they now have for these peasants, the fact that they visit them and take advantage of their vacations to go there and spend time with the peasants, that they are concerned, waiting to see whether or not the school has been built, and so forth, I ask myself, "Isn't this deeply Christian? Isn't this what Christ would want for the people of Nicaragua, that people in the city be concerned about their brothers and sisters in the country, that people in the city love people in the country, and that country people show their rural culture to city people and both sides appreciate each other's values?"

I think a young person in Nicaragua today can't ignore different ideological currents.

—*Contrary to this vision of yours and this Christian motivation you have, some groups of Christians, clergy, and bishops, are raising objections, protests, and accusations about the revolution's proposals for education. They accuse the leaders of being just the opposite of Christian, of being Marxist and of promoting an ideology that will take the people's faith away.*

—I've always asked them to show how the official plans and programs instill ideology and push atheism. We are encouraging pluralism and academic freedom, but we believe a young person in Nicaragua in this day and age can't be ignorant of Marxism, of socialism, just as he or she shouldn't be ignorant of social democracy, Christian democracy, liberalism, conservativism, or indeed any ideological current. What's really going on is that there are people who still have the mindset from Somoza's time, an anticommunist mindset that sees the devil in any pamphlet or any text where Marxism is mentioned or explained. Marxism is not opposed to Christianity in its analysis of social problems, in its analysis of the causes of the exploitation that has gone on over the ages, in the theory of surplus value, in class struggle, in fact, in a whole series of contributions that provide us with a basis for a scientific analysis of social phenomena. I've even come to the point where I think that when Marxism speaks of matter as the origin of everything, the Christian could accept it as God using matter so as to create a long process of evolution leading up to the situation in which humankind finds itself today.

I don't think it would be fruitful to get all wrapped up in an unending discussion, in a polemic on this point, but rather we should recognize that the kinds of social transformations that Marxism is aiming at are quite in agreement with Christian values.

I should tell you that when we are criticized this way for what we are doing in education, what's often behind these criticisms is a political and sectarian aim. For example, the National Literacy Crusade was criticized because it was said that the Crusade was going to "domesticate" the peasants or "make communists" out of them. What the Crusade did was to open the peasants' minds to show them their own reality, to teach them reading and writing as part of the revolutionary political process. There can't be any teaching to read and write except in a context. You can't teach reading and writing in a vacuum. All literacy work, like all education, is connected to a political process. There's no such thing as neutral education.

In the National Literacy Crusade we couldn't go to the peasants and teach them to read and write without telling them that a revolution had been victorious, without explaining that this revolution was seeking such-and-such aims, without explaining what agrarian reform is, without explaining the government's health programs, without saying, for example, that this government completely recognizes freedom of worship—all that is in the literacy workbook. Teaching literacy had to be consciousness raising, and it will continue to be so because through it people become aware of reality. Obviously, those who advocate "neutral education" would have preferred that peasants not learn to read and write and become aware of their situation. So those who want to manipulate the peasants are those same fine people who have kept our citizens in ignorance for centuries. According to their ideology it is better for the peasant to remain ignorant.

> **I pray with my wife every night and we read and discuss the Bible with our children once a week.**

—*You say you are a Christian in your revolutionary commitment, a practicing Catholic. I'm going to ask a very personal question. Besides publicly practicing your religion in your group or in the church's liturgy, do you practice personal prayer?*

—I pray with my wife every night. And we try to pray with all the family together once a week. When we are all together at lunchtime we have a Bible reading and then we may discuss it, or on weekends we have a Bible reading and all our children can say something and offer their contribution and then also have a little criticism and self-criticism. Sometimes my children are very critical toward me. Sometimes they criticize me for not conversing enough with them.

Your life is so busy that you're so involved in work that often you don't have much time to know your children's problems and concerns. They feel I'm very involved with my work at the ministry and that I should reserve more time for them.

—*Tell me a little about your family.*

—My wife's name is Rosa Carlota Pereira Bernheim. Fortunately we're very happy and enjoy our family life. We're a lot like each other in our character and we like many of the same things. We have seven children ranging from one who is 21 years old to one who just turned two. We have children in the university and next year the youngest will go into pre-school. My wife is also a Christian. We both belong to the Christians in the Revolution movement. We both agree with the idea that we can remain Christians within the revolution and that we Christians have an important contribution to make in this process. We believe that the greatest mistake a Christian could make would be to drop out of the revolutionary process and leave the country, flee from the revolution, since the presence of Christians in the revolution is what assures us that Christian values will remain in evidence and be important, giving the revolution its uniqueness, its own character. That is just what has made our revolution so attractive for everyone, for the whole world. It is a unique revolution, and it should keep its uniqueness, its originality, without ever becoming a servile copy of any other model. The active participation of Christians is part of this originality, this authenticity.

—*I'm finding out that the revolution has broken into and cut across many families, inevitably causing splits because people opt in different directions. What has been the impact on your family?*

—Fortunately in our family the revolution hasn't produced any split. My children, all those who were old enough, took part in the National Literacy Crusade. Taking part in the Crusade was very important for them. They matured and became more committed. Two of them are in the militia.

I want to point out one thing: in our family meetings we critically analyze the process, since I believe that the Christian's participation in the process shouldn't be an uncritical one. We Christians should keep watch to see that the revolution continues to proceed in accordance with the values that make it an example to the world. That's why we have criticism and self-criticism when we get together. This is important, since constructive criticism, made from the viewpoint of the poor and from the angle of authentic revolution, strengthens the revolution. It is healthy for the revolution to have inside it people who are keeping watch to see that it doesn't move away from its basic objectives. That will help it become firmly established and irreversible.

—*This synthesis of Christianity and living the revolution critically leads me to ask you about your early Christian education.*

—I was educated by the Christian Brothers. But I would emphasize that the motivating force in my Christian formation was not what I got from texts that sometimes had to be memorized. The Christian teaching that left the biggest impact on me was the example of some of the brothers whom I saw as exceptional. I thought that if these great teachers were Christians, then Christianity had to be something really exceptional. They had left their countries, come to Nicaragua, and devoted themselves to this country. So more than any teaching of a formal sort, the decisive thing for me was the example of some of these brothers. Then there was the fact that in my family we also had people whose Christian lives were exceptional. First, there was the example of my mother, who had to bear all the responsibility for the family as my father was sick for over ten years. She's the person who has influenced me the most.

My mother's twin sister, my aunt Cleotilde, was an Immaculate Conception nun. I remember when I was a child we used to go visit her in the sisters' school in Diriamba. I was very impressed by their conversation, their kindness, their poverty, their love for the children, their devotion. It may be that these examples provided my basic education and formation.

Above all, there's my burning interest in the life of Jesus. For me there's nothing more consuming than the life of Jesus, Jesus as human being and as son of God, but especially in the aspect of his being the most precious fruit humankind has produced. My Christianity is based on Jesus himself: the Jesus of the poor of the earth, who was born in a stable; the Jesus who is human and divine, human being and son of God. I have a great deal of admiration for his word, for his example, for everything that goes into Christ's life among human beings. Next to the life of Christ, the other life I've always considered extraordinary is that of Francis of Assisi. I think that of all the people in this world, he's the one who has come closest to the paradigm of Christ. The life of brother Francis of Assisi, brother to all people and to all things, has always impressed me. His sayings are the highest poem to humility and love of neighbor.

I get the impression the minister has emphasized the joys and satisfactions of his work and has passed over many of his crosses in silence. This ministry is something of a Calvary because some sectors in private education and Catholic education actively oppose the revolutionary reforms in education. With each reform, with each battle, Tünnermann, as Minister of Education comes forth to speak with his careful statements and studied calmness.

4

MARÍA DEL SOCORRO GUTIÉRREZ DE BARRETO

General Secretary of the Ministry of Housing

"I'm in the revolution because of my Christian faith; in it I can live the gospel better"

Born in San Juan del Sur on December 20, 1938, María del Socorro Gutiér-
rez is married to José Barreto. They have six children. She and her husband
were among the founders of the Christian Family Movement and did apostolic

work for it between 1963 and 1965. In 1966, she attended the first Cursillo de Cristiandad held for women in Managua. Until 1979 she was a cursillo leader. Now she belongs to Christians in the Revolution. Since July 17, 1979, she has been General Secretary of the Ministry of Housing and Human Settlement.

●

María del Socorro has large eyes and chestnut hair. There is a touch of care and elegance in her face and in her clothing.

Her house is spread out. From the outside it has something of both Andalusia and Castile. Posts of dark wood along a corridor stand out against the wrinkled white of the wall and lead to an inner patio. On the wall I notice keys, groups of keys, a small exposition of very old keys.

Inside, there is a pleasant dining room. Through the window I see a broad patio, green and closed-in, a natural sort of garden with a lawn and flowers, a cluster of fruit trees, and some dwarf palm trees with fan-shaped branches.

She has brought me here after work to record the interview. Night is falling.

●

Q—Tell me about your participation in the struggle of the Nicaraguan people. How did you awaken to the need to get involved and what actions did you take part in?

Gutiérrez—My role has always been to support from the rear guard. I became aware little by little, through the impact of many experiences. My father is a doctor and my mother devoted herself to the home. Both gave their all in order to give us, my brother and me, an easy life. In a family atmosphere like that, through the generosity of my father, who took care of people of all economic levels, but especially poor people, I discovered that there was poverty in my country. The result of it all was that as I grew up I had a concern that impelled me to look for answers. For me, the starting point was the Cursillo de Cristiandad, where I discovered more fully God the Father and the Christ who became incarnate with a love that was effective. Out of that love, I sought to analyze things in real life, the neighbor who was in need, social injustice in the structures of the system. I began to see with my own eyes all these real and terrible things in life that I had never analyzed before. Something had to be done.

In our group and in different Christian communities, we began to reflect on violence and nonviolence in connection with Christian faith. Our hierarchy made pronouncements in defense of our people, because it was clear that bombs were falling and killing people. But they always pointed to the danger of violence from both right and left equally, even when violence had been institutionalized since before the bombs began to fall. Those guidelines led some groups of Christians to drop back and not support the revolutionary cause so as not to foment what, as violence, was considered wrong and unfitting for Christians, even when it was for the defense of the people.

Another group of Christians, among whom I count myself, saw that the unjust violence was Somoza's and all the machinery of death he used against our people. That population had awakened and was defending itself against Somoza's unjust violence. It was logical and even necessary for the people to defend themselves with vigor, with violence. There was no other way for them to defend themselves, and that is why their violence against Somoza's murderous and unjust violence was legitimate. It was just and was an ethical duty, a duty of Christian love for the whole population that was subject to oppression and repression. The people of the Sandinista Front, who had come out of years of struggle for liberation, who were surrounded by a great mystique and were willing to sacrifice their own lives, were the vanguard leading the anti-Somoza struggle, defending the legitimate interests of the people: the right to live and the right to set up an overall project for the people, one worthy of human beings. Later when the armed insurrection was an undeniable fact, the bishops also legitimized it as something just.

My brother's suffering in prison made me feel the drama of the young people who were in jail and of their mothers and families.

—In October 1977 they put my brother in jail. Those were days of wrenching pain. For three weeks we had no idea whether he was alive or dead. And again the contrasts had a big impact on me. My brother, an upright doctor with many fine personal qualities, esteemed in his profession, received a lot of attention from the media when he was arrested. His whole family was working on his behalf, and in fact we stopped our regular work in order to try to get him out of jail. But the other prisoners didn't have anyone. Every day we were in international contact with medical associations and asked them to make statements on behalf of my brother. We got excellent responses and they were a big help in making sure his life was respected. During the long lonely nights, I wondered about the suffering of the mothers of the guerrillas and of the young people who were put in jail in Managua and the other cities just because they were suspected of being Sandinistas. They didn't have lawyer friends to call on as we did. On those grey afternoons, seated on the floor of the hallway of the court, I felt committed to all the young people who were in jail.

At that time we experienced rejection from so many people, many of them people whom we'd held in high esteem. They kept their distance from us as though we were lepers, because my brother was in jail for working with the Sandinistas.

When we were being bombed, I decided that if I lived through it I would have to give everything for my people.

—*How did you take part in the people's struggle during the war and the final insurrection?*

—What we had to offer was our work and our home. Pepe, my husband, had a photography studio and he developed film. They asked us to help by letting our house be used for meetings of some members of the group of the Twelve and as a place to hide. It meant risks, but after talking it over in the family we decided that it was our moral and Christian obligation to do as we had been asked.

In our weekly meetings of prayer and reflection on the Word of God—the light by which we examined the situations we were experiencing—my Christian community confirmed my decision to support my people's struggle.

My house had become a hiding place or safe house for the *muchachos*. Each time they left, I felt a little like a mother to each one of them, and as we were saying good-bye, we often prayed together. I always told them that at the hardest moments in the struggle, during the greatest risks or when they felt most isolated, they would never be alone, because the Lord would be with them and a whole church would be in constant prayer for them. When they went away, I used to think that they might never return, that they might fall in the struggle. They were giving their life to liberate their people. That did a great deal to fortify my decision to work for this revolution.

Late one tragic afternoon—they had been bombing the eastern part of the city from ten in the morning until four in the afternoon—we got together, Carlos, Vidaluz, my parents, my husband, and myself. That afternoon I felt a reaffirmation of my duty to do everything to contribute toward raising up this people if we came out of that alive. I compared what I had done with what I could have done. I realized I was in a neighborhood that was protected, and in a house that was safer and more comfortable than people in other neighborhoods. And I reaffirmed that if I got out alive I had to give the rest of my life for my people.

On July 20, 1979 [the day after the Sandinista victory], my parents and I went to get my brother Juan Ignacio. My father wept silently. We all embraced one another. I was overwhelmed by the enthusiasm of the crowds in the streets and by the arrival of the young people who had fought. What struck me most was that we didn't see older people—almost all of them were very young. And I said to myself, "This country of ours is in the hands of the youth. It is a people that has just been born and will have to grow up through a process of education that will be long, hard, and costly."

Tell me if the revolution has changed your Christian life.

—The revolution means a big change for us. It has made us insert our ideal of changing our lives into the real human history of our people. Changing our lives now becomes something concrete when we leave behind us a whole series of things, advantages and privileges. I gave up my work in the private sector. We have given up a business we had, and now we have thrown ourselves into a kind of responsibility and service we've not been used to.

Being within the revolution enables me to see clearly that this process is aimed at raising up the oppressed, the weak, the poor. Through my faith, which comes from the gospel (Luke 4), I make my contribution to the revolution with my work in the Ministry of Housing and Human Settlement. For example, when lands are apportioned within the program for reorganizing city land, the aim is to relocate families who used to live on the banks of Lake Managua, where the city's sewer waters empty (a very polluted situation), or along riverbanks where large numbers of people had put up their houses since they couldn't get land because of the high price. They were piled up there and there was a great deal of sickness and danger during the rainy seasons, since the water would rush down the streambeds and wash their houses away and put them in danger.

The revolution is moving family groups to the best lands in the city. Any visitor can see in Managua and other cities quite close to some houses of rich families, other little huts, made with just a few boards put together, some with new lumber but most with old boards. We've taken the first step, which is getting the land, and that means a secure future and a healthier environment, which will lower infant mortality. We are confident that we will be able to improve the houses. By the end of 1982 land had been given free to 6,000 families. To do so, we used a Law for Expropriating Unused Urban Lands, taking over empty lots in order to benefit thousands of people who were living in unfit conditions. The reason for the move was a deeply human one, one of love (and where there is love, God is there). Brigades of volunteers from the Sandinista Youth, from the Sandinista Popular Army, from the mass organizations, from the Housing Ministry and other ministries, all went there. They worked in the rain and helped people organize their moving. Today these communities are organizing themselves so they can continue to improve their living conditions.

For me, sharing in the hope of those who get a parcel of land free is one way of putting the preferential option for the poor into practice. That way my faith has become incarnate; it has become concrete in the practice of love. Even if someone comes here to the Ministry with a need we can't meet at the moment, even though I can't solve that person's problem right away, I know that there is an overall plan underway that is aimed at solving this problem and all the rest, and that that plan is moving ahead. My experience is that by being incarnated here, my faith picks up strength, it becomes realistic and effective.

Our salaries are low. We've gone over to living like the people who live off their work and have nothing to spare.

—You say you left your job, your business in the private sector, and have committed yourselves to working to serve this revolutionary project. What I see is that you and other people in your Christian group now have jobs with the state. Isn't there something of a new kind of opportunism here?

—It doesn't seem to me that there's any opportunism on our part. There has been a sincere conversion, through faith, to the option for the poor. Economically, we've gone over to living with the austerity of the employees of the revolutionary state, and that means we share the experience of most of our people who have lived from their work and nothing else, with nothing to spare. Today, we have nothing to spare, no savings. The salaries of state employees are low, and they have to be that way. As I experience this, I recall that passage in the gospel where it tells us, "Do not be overconcerned with what you will wear, nor with what you will eat; seek the kingdom of God and his justice, and the rest will be yours in abundance."

All the remaining time that the tasks and work of the revolution allows us, we spend in work and services related to the church. That means forming our communities and coordinating with the grassroots Christian communities.

—Do Christians have something of their own to contribute to the revolution?

—I think the first thing Christians contribute should be a love that is persistent. And then there is critical analysis from the perspective of that Christian love. Sometimes those of us who are immersed in activity can forget the perspective of the other. And you can forget to live out that love toward the other person in tolerance, understanding, forgiveness, in helping, and in providing new opportunities. I believe the challenge to us Christians in Nicaragua is for this love to remain alive and active in this revolutionary process, which is subject to so many daily frictions. Love should remain, even in the midst of the vigorous and firm measures we sometimes have to take to defend ourselves.

What I see in the Sandinista Popular Militias and in the Reserve Infantry Battalions is that our young people are full of hope as they go to defend our homeland, and their motivation is not that of hate or revenge, but of love— they are going to defend life. Today the murderous Guard, under whose repression our people suffered for over forty years, are cruelly kidnapping and killing peasants, cutting off their heads. They are continuing their antilife activity. But our combatants are struggling for life. What I see there is a living expression of love. They are heroic because they are risking their lives. Nevertheless certain sectors of the church put them down or reject them and use words like "hatred" or "militarism" just because they are defending and strengthening the revolution. These sectors neither see nor denounce the hatred in the cruel actions of the counterrevolutionary bands. And when it comes to daily crimes and murder against the peasants and those citizens who volunteer to go and pick coffee, our hierarchy remains silent. What does this mean? How are we to interpret it?

Another great contribution of Christians, a projection of their love, is forgiveness. Also the contribution of their work in different sectors and levels of the revolution at the service of the people, motivated by the gospel.

—You hear fears and accusations about those Christians who are involved in this process, which, according to those accusations, is heading toward totalitarianism, toward Marxism—Leninism, toward atheism. . . .

—Deep down, I think the truth of the matter is this: this process aims to better the situation and the life of the poor, and there is a cost for all of us who previously enjoyed higher living standards. From a Christian perspective I say, "I have to lose in order to share." I have to share all I have, my whole life.

> **I've not had the least problem with my faith and my freedom in this revolutionary process.**

—Where is this process heading? Toward totalitarianism and toward the dark clouds described in some accusations? That depends on us. It depends on all of us, because the process is something all of us are doing. We Christians are in the revolution to keep it from going in the wrong direction. That's one more reason why Christians should be active in the process.

I should say that up to this point I don't see the process headed toward totalitarianism. I've not had the least problem with my faith and my freedom in the process. I'm going to tell you about some of my personal feelings and how I got over them. Right after the revolutionary victory, the demonstrations of the people upset me because of the language they used. Especially because of some rough slogans you would hear, yelling "Firing squad!" and things like that. Only as the process went on did I gradually realize that the people had just had a muzzle taken off, one that had kept them suffering in silence for decades, and naturally they couldn't be expected to use all the proper expressions. They were getting things out of their system.

When I had gotten to this point, one day, feeling quite apprehensive, I joined a demonstration heading toward the Plaza of the Revolution. I saw lots of women with misshapen feet, their faces prematurely aged. I looked at myself and saw the contrast. I saw my own feet protected by good shoes next to other feet that were bare and cracked, covered with dust as though they were rooted in the earth, feet where you could see the blood pumping through gnarled varicose veins. There alongside these women I felt deeply rooted in the people. Even though I didn't know them by name, we all shared and loved something that had just been saved, our own identity. I could recognize hope in so many eyes, and being there with my people I felt very close to the Lord. I asked him to give me light and strength to help in building a new history of justice and equality, despite my weaknesses and limitations, so as not to defraud the hopes of so many people.

I'm not blind to the mistakes that have been made and might be made. Like all human processes, this one is liable to make mistakes. It's being pushed, harassed, and destabilized—to force it to make more mistakes—by American imperialism, and by the sectors of the bourgeoisie and of the church who join in the destabilization efforts. But as long as I see that the errors are relative and don't affect the process as a whole in its orientation toward the poor, I support it. The day the revolution is not oriented toward the poor, I'll be the first to feel it must be denounced. But as long as it is oriented—and we orient it—toward the good of the poor majority, I'm going to live the gospel within that process.

Several times I've seen María del Soccorro taking part in meetings of Christians, and going here and there seeking dialogue with the bishops. It is as though she were following out a charism to promote communion in the midst of all the tensions and conflicts.

5

EDGARDO GARCÍA

General Secretary of the Association of Rural Workers

**"I've never divorced the workers' struggle
from my struggle as a Christian"**

Born January 11, 1956, in San Gregorio, Diriamba, Edgardo García attended school while he also worked tending cattle and went into high school while he was working in a textile factory. In 1974 he became connected to the

FSLN, and led the struggles of workers on the coffee plantations of Carazo. In 1975 he started the first Juntas Comunales *[organizations of local elected government]. In 1976 he became involved in the organized rural pastoral work of the Catholic Church and became part of the movement of the Celebrators of the Word. He helped organize the Committees of Rural Workers, which were semilegal union organizations. In 1978 he was elected General Secretary of the Association of Rural Workers (ATC). He was reelected as General Secretary at the second assembly, which followed the revolutionary victory. His is a Sandinista and a member of the National Assembly. In 1981, he was named coordinator of the Coordinating Body of Unions of Nicaragua (CSN).*

●

He has come to the place I suggested we meet, preferring to get out of his office. "That way they won't interrupt us." He wears the blue cap commonly worn in Nicaragua as a protection against the tropical sun and wind.

He is short and strong, serious but good-natured. At twenty-six, he radiates a vigor that has been seasoned by ten years of intense struggle. His face is brown and sharp, as though chiseled.

I grew up tending cattle, in a religious atmosphere where there were both Catholics and Protestants.

Q—Where did you live before the revolution? What did you do?

García—I grew up in my own district, out there, and worked tending cattle. I took care of the animals, the cattle belonging to my grandfathers on both sides, until I was thirteen. While doing that kind of work, I also went to school. I got up to sixth grade in the school in my district. Then I went on to try to go to high school, combining it with work in a textile factory.

—How was your Christian life and formation throughout those years?

—I come from a Catholic family. Catechists used to come to the district, young people, novices, or something like that, to prepare children between seven and twelve years old for their first communion. I took part in that. Also, my father—I didn't live with him all the time but I used to visit him—my father is a Baptist pastor. My world was full of religious life, both through my grandparents, who raised me, and through my father. Besides that, in the district there are people who belong to other sects, and I had good relations with them. Sometimes I went outside the district with workers who belonged to some sect and I took part in their ceremonies and practices. With Catholics I took part in things toward the end of the year, Christmas, *La Purísima*, Holy Week and other acts of faith that people practice out in the country.

—*But you stayed with the Catholic Church.*

—That's right. I was always friendly with everybody but I stayed with the Catholic Church.

He parcels out his words with a peasant's slowness and deliberation. Sure and firm, like someone working with a hoe, stroke by stroke, row by row, word by word, sentence by sentence. I realize the rhythm and language of this interview are quite different from the other interviews. It is plain from his speech what class Edgardo comes from. With few words and in little time, he will give his testimony with that peasant wisdom that fills Nicaragua's Christianity and its revolution.

The fact that a kind of Christianity dealing with human suffering was being preached got me interested and I became a Delegate of the Word among the peasants.

—In the Catholic Church I came to participate in the group of the Celebrators of the Word, which was made up of peasants who received some theological formation. The fact is that I would have come to the point where it wouldn't matter to me whether people were Catholics or Protestants, which religion wouldn't matter to me. I was practically at that point, but I felt drawn to a kind of preaching that was committed to the poor, a preaching that took up social problems. So when I came to make my own decisions, it was in this line of commitment, of a willingness to struggle alongside the workers, the poor.

—*Where and when did you become interested in the preaching of a Christianity committed to the poor?*

—That was in 1973. Around December, I was invited by a group of Christians in the parish of Diriamba. They were going to a place that belonged to Caritas [a social agency of the church—TRANS.]. There I met Father Uriel Molina, who made a theological presentation, and took up the question of the earthquake. He said, "It's not just a question of nature. There are other things that should be shaken up here, what should be shaken up is the consciousness of those who allow themselves to be held in subjection, and the pride of those who oppress them should be brought down." He gave some explanation. He took up the whole question of the earthquake and all the dirty tricks that were being played, tricks like pocketing the aid that came from other countries, or the way the powerful of that period got more prestige out of the hunger the people were enduring.

This time I had met a priest who was different, someone who was not repeating the same old things, about whether something was a sin or wasn't, about whether I was guilty or not, whether God was looking at me or not looking at me. This time it wasn't anything like that, but it was dealing with the cause of human suffering. It was dealing with the cause of the pride of the powerful, and also their blindness, you see, and also with the way those who submit to slavery are really asleep. It was different. At that point, I began to feel that this way, this way of practicing the faith, was a way that meant that if you had to suffer, it would be for things that were real. For things that were real. Not because of some strange spirits hovering over your mind, but because of the presence of real human beings who were suffering hunger and exploitation, you see. That was why. So that was when I began to get interested.

Then I got to listening to two priests on the radio, Alfonso Alvarado and Leonel Navas. They came here to a station and out where I was; I listened to what they had to say and also found it interesting.

Before that time, I had been working in a factory. After the earthquake, I went into a textile factory, and there I was struggling along with my coworkers, and we went on strike. I had previously made contact with a woman in the Sandinista Front, but she had to go away for military training and I was left without any contact. We lost the strike and they fired me from that factory. With my own concern for social commitment and my faith in change, when I heard those priests, I began to look into how I could get connected with them. I did that through CEPA, which extended a kind of training for peasants. It was to support the rural pastoral work going on at the time and many parishes took part. Although the parish in Diriamba, where I was, didn't take part, we used to go over to the parish in San Marcos, where the priest was supporting that kind of training.

After leaving the factory, I went back to the countryside. But I no longer felt any attraction for growing crops or for just settling down in my own little house. That looked like sweating to produce things that wouldn't benefit me or those who lived with me. There had to be another way out. And I began to try to do some organizing. We organized some District Juntas. In the District Juntas we were concerned with solving the problems of community services, safe drinking water, electricity, services, health centers, schools, learning some craft things, you see, a whole series of activities. In order to strengthen this community struggle there had to be the element of faith. We had to foment a committed kind of religious practice. That was where I became a Delegate of the Word.

> **We combined struggle and Christian faith. The Word of God illuminated and strengthened the peasant struggle.**

—I was active as a Delegate of the Word from the time I was sixteen until I was nineteen. At first it was all a matter of learning how to use the Bible right, to get to know the Word of God, and then how to lead meetings, celebrations, religious ceremonies, to try to read a message where there were specific guidelines, or case studies that drew us into the reality we were experiencing. We always made an effort to reinforce the overall aim of unifying the communities through organization. We had to find the causes of sin, of exploitation, of backwardness, and to support development projects.

I didn't have much of a problem in learning to use the Bible, because I had a good deal of experience. But finding a new way of explaining it in order to apply it to our situation did take some time.

Gradually, with some struggle, we managed to get the District Juntas for Development going, and the Movement of Celebrators of the Word, and a cooperative or so, where peasants were working together planting fruits or grains. And in all these ways of organizing we were supporting the struggles of rural workers, those who were laborers on the coffee haciendas.

When other kinds of organizations began to suffer repression, denunciation of the system was kept alive through the celebration of the Word of God. The Word of God shed light on and strengthened the whole struggle of the people in the countryside, the peasants, the rural workers. By their faith in God, they found reasons to struggle for their rights. They used to say, "OK, maybe I'm not brave enough to take up arms, but I will be brave enough not to do like Peter, not to betray the cause that the best of our nation's young people are struggling for, strength enough not to turn anyone in." Christian faith and the struggle were combined there.

—*How was this struggle connected to the overall struggle against the system and to the Sandinista struggle?*

—There came a point when, besides the religious work, union organizing was going on. In that work we had underground organizations and semiunderground organizations. The underground organizations were almost party organizations, practically Sandinista, you could say. There came a time when we could say to someone, "OK, *compañero,* this is the Sandinista Front. The group that's running all this, that's planning and managing it, is the Sandinista Front." We used to plan our organizing work from within the Sandinista Front. The religious work was something that belonged to the religious movement in the communities, celebrating their assemblies and all that. We used to come to ask the assembly of Christians for their help and collaboration, for example, when there was a land occupation. Then the Christians would arrange to celebrate a meeting or assembly of support or make a statement when people's rights had been trampled. In fact, they sometimes occupied the churches. The Celebrators of the Word went to the churches and occupied them. There was a whole series of things where the organizing and unionizing work with peasants was combined with the activity of Christian movements in their assemblies, in their own particular practices.

Everyone knew I was a Christian committed to the Sandinista struggle to the end.

—I was involved in this form of struggle until 1976, when the bishops denounced the government and wrote the pastoral letter on the murder and violent disappearance of peasants in the northern mountains.* Up to that point I took part in the celebration of the Word and was a religious leader. We had a big push on courses for teaching peasants to read and write. But afterwards, in 1977, they were really after me. By that time, for me to take part in an open meeting with Christians was a big problem. Often if I went to the church they recognized me both as a Celebrator of the Word and as a Sandinista leader. Everyone knew I was a Christian who was committed to the Sandinista struggle to the end. So I had to go underground.

From that time onward, given the kind of role and responsibility I was taking on, one that could only be clandestine, I devoted myself mainly to union organizing, and to preparing logistical support for the guerrillas, with all the Christian contacts I had in the countryside. All those who were Celebrators of the Word with me, people who got together to share their faith—we were no longer living this practice openly but underground—they all helped me with logistical support for the guerrillas. They helped by supporting the struggle for land. They made commentaries in their celebrations, the same sorts of commentaries we had always made, but bringing the congregation up to date with each new struggle the people took on. That's how I kept up my connection, underground, because by that time, for all practical purposes, I was a guerrilla.

That's how we went along, getting conditions ready for the insurrection, with this whole support network of Celebrators of the Word, union members, cooperative members, and rural workers.

—*Where were you, and what was your experience during the insurrection?*

—During the war I was assigned to a part of the internal front, in Carazo, my area, where I was born. I was in charge of union leadership there. That meant I was responsible for logistical support in the countryside. My task was to get the unions or the workers on each plantation to take over running the plantation in the middle of the war. It was my job to make sure the peasants in

---

*The Capuchin priests denounced the torture and mass murders of peasants in northern Nicaragua in 1976. Beginning in 1977, over two years, the Conference of Bishops issued a series of pastoral letters denouncing the dictatorship and supporting the people's right to struggle.—ED.

the liberated zones planted food crops even though the war was going on. Besides that, I had to get support for the guerrilla forces and strengthen and lead peasant troops, make sure they stayed in order, and get others to join the militias. I moved all over the countryside doing these activities. For example, we were put in charge of preventing troops from other areas from getting to Somoza's Guard to reinforce them. We were trying to get the Guard out of Diriamba. That was mainly what my work was. I was part of the leadership of the militias.

—Was there any moment when your life was in danger?

—You could say I was in serious danger twice. One time I had to go into the city to make some contacts and get some information about where the enemy forces were. When I did that I often found myself in a difficult situation because they used to give me ammunition to take back to the countryside. And of course I had to act very friendly and cheerful despite all the danger. So one day, I was going out on horseback and they caught me. At that point I thought I was going to die—they'd kill me for transporting ammunition. But I made believe I was a father who had to take food to his children. I practically cried. The Guardsmen didn't reach down into the bag of beans; there were bullets down there. They took a look, saw they were beans, and didn't reach down. So I got out of that one.

On another occasion, they stopped me here, leaving the National Seminary. We'd had a meeting. I was carrying a notebook with the conclusions of the meeting of the national body of the ATC, the Association of Rural Workers. And I also had some articles from the paper we published, *El Machete.* They made me raise my hands up against the jeep while they looked at this notebook. I also had a Bible. I presented myself as a Christian—that's what I am. So they began to take a look. They were searching for abbreviations and messages. But the only thing they found in initials was ATC. So they said, "What the hell's this?" So I said, "That's Activity of Christianity." "But what's this in the middle?" they said, "What does this mean?" "Ah," I said to them, "that's the sign of the Christian, the "T," like the cross."

He bursts out laughing.

—Naturally there were other times when the struggle was risky.

I've never divorced the workers' struggle from my struggle as a Christian.

—Throughout this struggle, what did Christian faith mean to you?

—Really, I've never divorced one thing from the other. I've never divorced the various kinds of struggle, whether the struggle to reveal and denounce the hypocrisy of the exploiters, the struggle to fortify the unity and organization of the workers, the struggle to eliminate the mechanisms of exploitation and the mechanisms for murder that the exploiters organize, the struggle to experience together with the poor their love and faith in their religious practices. I don't disconnect these struggles from the life of the Christian. I've never looked at it as two things. Christian faith has always been a part of me in every struggle.

—*There was a victory. Where has your work gone since then?*

—Since before that victory, I've been committed to the rural workers, the poor and humble, and to Christians. In terms of sectors in society, I was committed to the agricultural workers of Nicaragua. That commitment led me to take on that task formally, and today I'm general secretary of the ATC. They appointed me even before victory when the ATC was organized.

—*Does it extend to all agricultural workers in the country?*

—It extends to farm workers, to wage laborers. That doesn't keep me from taking part in acts that express the faith, along with other Christians. But because of my position it is impossible for me to exercise the role I used to have as Celebrator of the Word. Why? Because I often have to explain on a national level, over the media, the tasks we have to accomplish as rural workers. One part of the hierarchy might look badly on that, and they could say we want to destroy their flock if I continued to be a Celebrator of the Word. They see me laying down guidelines as the General Secretary of the ATC.

—*Is the ATC an organ of the Sandinista Party?*

—It's a farm workers organization that recognizes the Sandinista Front as its revolutionary vanguard. It represents Sandinista organizing of one sector of the Nicaraguan working class. We are heading toward being integrated in one central union federation, which would embrace unions organized according to sectors. In it we would be a national union, the National Union of Agricultural Workers of Nicaragua.

There's no point in providing the enemy of the poor and of the revolution with weapons. That's why I can't be a leader in the celebration as I used to be, but I can take part as a Christian. I attend and I do take part.

—*What is your ordinary working day like?*

—I get up at six or before. I exercise for a half hour, and then get washed. By seven or seven-thirty, I'm in the office. I read the papers until eight, and I set aside any particularly interesting article for the evening. Normally during the morning I have working meetings. I also receive journalists. I check with the provinces about particular cases of conflict or work. I have lunch at one. During the afternoon I devote myself to special commissions that are gathering and analyzing information or checking work projects we're developing. Part of the afternoon is used to coordinate with colleagues in other national unions. All this takes up to six-thirty. Then there are activities with institutions, conferences, assemblies, visits from friendly organizations in other countries, having supper with them. That goes on until nine. Then before going to sleep I read articles or some book I'm interested in and go over the next day's agenda. I go to sleep around midnight.

That's a normal office day. It's different when I go out to the grassroots around the country. I make eight ordinary visits a month to local organizations out in the provinces.

—*Do you still feel like a Christian and outwardly profess your Christianity?*

—I am a Christian. I am a Christian who is identified with this movement. I feel that a good part of my roots are there. I am a Christian in order to live the Christianity I chose. Because as I said at the beginning I saw many currents of Christianity that didn't satisfy me. But this one did. So I participate in the kind of Christianity I chose.

—*And you don't find that any aspects of revolutionary Sandinista militancy put limits on your faith and your Christian conscience?*

—No, I don't feel that. For example, in regard to the problem of ideology, of theory, OK, so there are some folks who are Sandinistas and believe in historical materialism and in dialectical materialism. It's no problem for me if they want to believe in that. No problem. In fact it's clear to me that many Christians have been a part of bringing that person not to believe in Christ. We could say that that person who does not believe in Christ, in his or her commitment to the poor, has done more than those who spend their lives striving to make people believe in Christ and yet don't lift a finger for the struggle of the poor.

—*From your experience, what do you think of those who accuse the revolutionary process and* Sandinismo *of intending to make things atheistic, of persecuting religion and the church?*

—The fact is that those who do not have the moral authority to defend their faith in positive terms have to use threats. There are people here, very wealthy people, who have been involved in prostitution, in drug traffic, who have exploited and destroyed others. Obviously their God is in their wallet, since, as the gospel says, "Where your treasure is, there also will your heart be." So the position of many of these Christians who feel afraid of revolutionary atheism really identifies them with counterrevolutionary atheism.

—*If I've understood you correctly, the great overlap or convergence of Christian faith and the revolutionary process for you means commitment to the poor, the option for the poor.*

—Well, not in my case, since I'm also poor. In my case the overlap between Christianity and Sandinismo is that both take on the desire and the power of the poor to liberate themselves. Both have faith in that power and both have based themselves on that power of the poor to free themselves, to achieve liberation. I couldn't say I make the option for the poor since I'm poor myself.

—*Your answer contains a good lesson. Tell me, Edgardo, are the farmworkers and peasants in Nicaragua Christians, are they religious?*

—Yes, certainly. Religion is very alive for Nicaraguan agricultural workers. The movement of the Celebrators of the Word grew very rapidly. In a year and a half it spread throughout the whole country, despite the repression and difficulties we've had to face.

I'd have to say that if the values of Christianity that are part of Nicaraguan farm workers are not taken into account and esteemed, the struggle of all of us workers will be harder. There is a great unity between the tasks that have to be done and respect for the faith that is part of us farm workers.

The office of the General Secretary of the ATC is simple, plain, bare, and poor, like peasant houses. I visit Edgardo there to take some final notes. He gives me a book on Agrarian Reform in the Nicaraguan Revolution in which he has an article on the history of the ATC, its origins, its activities, its present position, and its aspirations. This enables me to broaden what Edgardo has told me. I learn that the ATC has grown from 12,000 members before the revolutionary victory to 135,000 now. I learn how the farm workers have struggled against the flight of capital after 1979, and how the ATC views the Agrarian Reform: "It is not simply distributing land; for us the Agrarian Reform includes the cultural, intellectual, technical, social, and political transformation of the peasants, their being able to take part in discussing production plans, their political development and their intellectual development."

6

REINALDO ANTONIO TEFEL

Minister-President of the Institute of
Social Security and Welfare

**"I've always lived out my Christianity by being involved
in politics on the side of the people"**

*Reinaldo Tefel was born in Managua in 1925. He was long involved in the
anti-Somoza struggle and was close to events of the struggle, exile, imprison-
ment and torture of Pedro Joaquín Chamorro, who was murdered in 1979.*

From 1965 to 1972 he taught Latin American sociology, industrial social psychology, group dynamics, and the sociology of change at the university level. As a student he wrote Toward a New Republic. *In 1946 he founded and ran the political weekly* El Universitario. *Among his writings are* El Infierno de los Pobres *(1972), and* La Revolución Sandinista *(1979). He was a member of the FSLN and the Twelve. He married Gloria de la Rocha in 1946; they have three children.*

●

The minister has a spacious office. There are rugs on the floor and many paintings and photos on the walls of historic people and moments: Sandino, Carlos Fonseca, Pedro Joaquín Chamorro and himself in Somoza's prison, ordinary people suffering, shots of mothers and children reflecting their dire poverty.

Now after the workday, the minister has brought me to his house, which is hidden behind a wall of tall trees planted closely together forming a giant green shield. "We planted them ourselves twenty years ago."

In a pleasant and quiet room we talk, eat supper, and go back to talking. Gloria, his wife, is with us the whole time.

●

Tefel—From the time of the revolutionary victory my work has been to run the Nicaraguan Institute of Social Security. I found it completely bankrupt, disorganized, and undisciplined. It had all the vices of the Somoza era. From the beginning, we set out to de-Somozaize it and set it in order. In the second week we set up study and consciousness-raising groups for the whole staff. In small groups, right where they work, they discussed their role in the revolutionary process. Since then, we've been gradually improving the staff, their spirit, their work, and the service they give.

I had been working with the Junta in San José, Costa Rica.* I didn't want this job because it looked very technical to me. I wanted something more political and made that point to the Junta several times. But they said to me, "You've worked with the poor all your life. Now's your big chance." I accepted it, and now I wouldn't want to be switched to another job. Here I've managed to link the technical, the political, and the human all together, and the Institute has taken on a new spirit.

---

*In July 1979 during the final phase of the anti-Somoza struggle, the Sandinistas formed a Junta, or provisional government, in Costa Rica, which included FAO's Alfonso Robelo, Pedro Joaquín Chamorro's widow, Violeta, Sergio Ramírez and Miguel d'Escoto of the Twelve, and the FSLN's Daniel Ortega and Moisés Hassan.—ED.

The functions of the Ministry of Social Welfare, which was done away with, as a separate entity have been attached to this Institute, which now takes care of all aspects of social security and social welfare. It provides for the whole population and especially the large sectors of the most needy, families, old people, children.

I tell him that the slogan coined about the children of Nicaragua—"los mimados de la Revolución" [*those whom the revolution babies or spoils with privileges*]—*is very nice but that, to judge by what you can see in the streets of Managua, the revolution's favors haven't been successful in bringing those children out of poverty, or in keeping them from begging and missing school.*

—There's no question that there are horrible problems. There are at least six thousand children in the streets of Managua, selling newspapers, cleaning and watching cars, roaming around, stealing. We have a plan to bring them into the School/Work Program in four years. Nevertheless, these problems are structural and they won't go away until we get the economy going again and can change social and economic structures. When will we do that? Only in the long run. Perhaps in ten years we'll be getting to the point where we no longer see children in the streets. Also, it depends on whether they leave us in peace, and don't threaten us, or invade us, or blockade us, or strangle us with war and other destabilizing actions, like what's happening now.

—*Let's jump to another dimension of your life. You are a Christian and practice Christianity. What is your practice and your Christian involvement like now?*

—I conceive of my Christian involvement as working in the revolution and that's how I practice it. And I practice it where I am. This work is so absorbing that I don't have time for any other activity. As I see it, doing my duty as a Christian, responding to my Christian conscience, means working the best I can where I am. When I'm able and have time and a bit of inspiration, I write something with a Christian angle as a help for others.

Shortly after victory I got all the employees together and gave them a talk on the Sandinista People's Revolution and its main characteristics, and I emphasized the role we Christians have played in this revolution, a very important role. That's one of this revolution's unique features. This is the first real revolution, from the French Revolution until now, where there is significant and massive participation by Christians, and by Christians as such. Someone told me that there were Christians in the American Revolution. But they took part as liberals, not as Christians. That is, they didn't live their Christian awareness explicitly in the revolution, although they were vaguely inspired by Christianity. But in this revolution those of us who are Christian have participated and are participating clearly motivated by our Christian faith, and we've never tried to hide that.

My religious practice now really comes down to Mass on Saturday evening. They've asked me to participate in the Christians in the Revolution movement, but I can't because of my work, and even less now that I have to take it easy to recuperate from my illness.

It was my traditional Catholic education that led to political struggle.

—What route brought you to take part in revolutionary struggle?

—First I should tell you that that route of struggle started in my early Christian education. My schooling and religious formation was with the Christian Brothers—a traditional Catholic education. And yet it was precisely the religious formation I had that led me into the struggle. I felt it was my moral duty as a Christian to take part in the social and political struggle against injustice. When I was in high school, together with Pedro Joaquín Chamorro, Ernesto Cardenal, and Rafael Córdova Rivas, I organized a group of young people. Some were in the Pedagogical Institute with the Christian Brothers, others in Central America High School with the Jesuits, and others in a school named after Rubén Darío. Together we set up Nationalist Action, an organization that even then took a Sandinista and anti-imperialist position.

Then I was sent to study in the United States. I was with the Jesuits at Fordham in New York for two years. There my greatest influence came from Catholic and Christian writers like Maritain, Leon Bloy, Berdyaev, Mounier, and other writers like Dostoyevsky and Chesterton.

When I came back to Nicaragua and entered the Central University to study law, I started a weekly paper called *El Universitario*. That was the first weekly Sandinista paper published in Nicaragua. I'm talking about the period before 1950, between 1946 and 1948 to be exact. It was quite a revolutionary period. That paper sold more than any other in Nicaragua at that time. When the old Somoza, the one who killed Sandino, was still dictator, when no one dared to mention Sandino in Nicaragua, I devoted a whole issue of *El Universitario* to Sandino on the anniversary of his murder. The price I had to pay was exile. I went to Mexico and there I met up with Pedro Joaquín Chamorro, who was also in exile. That was in 1946, but I was in Mexico only two months. I went to Honduras and came back across the border in order to keep on struggling against the Somoza dictatorship.

Every step I took in the anti-Somoza struggle was inspired by my sense of democracy and my Christian faith.

—That struggle took place in the streets. I joined masses of people demonstrating, put up notices by night and slipped them under people's doors. Sometimes we would come out of the university in a demonstration and the people would join us until the Guardia broke it up with rifle butts, tear gas, and clubs. That was constantly happening until Somoza closed the university in Managua and ordered us students to go to León. Out of rebellion, I didn't go, but stayed in Managua. Some of us students, along with a group of professors, set up the Free University, which lasted one year.

During that period I started UNAP, the National Union of People's Action. They called us the *Unapistas*. It was a much more democratic and progressive movement than Nationalist Action, the group we had organized in high school. The first people I called to help set it up were Pedro Joaquín Chamorro and Arturo Cruz. The three of us started UNAP. Later Ernesto Cardenal, Rafael Córdova Rivas, and other people like that came in. Perhaps it was premature, too advanced for the time. The people were still very much in the hold of the traditional parties, the Conservative Party and the Liberal Party. At that time people called themselves Liberal or Conservative even though they didn't know what it meant. So our group was in fact an elite group. That's not what we wanted, but that's the way it was. And it was a movement with a Christian inspiration, quite influenced by Christian democracy and by Maritain.

While still a student in Matagalpa, Carlos Fonseca, later the founder and commander-in-chief of the Sandinista Front, belonged to UNAP. There was a movement called "April '54," an attempt at anti-Somoza revolution in which the UNAP members took part. I remember that Ernesto Cardenal and I—we were all soldiers in it—were sent to watch the U.S. embassy to see when Somoza came and sent word to La Loma because we wanted to attack him while he was inside. The plot failed and so I had to spend more than a year underground. When I came out, the first two people who came to greet me, with no connection between them, were Ernesto Cardenal and Carlos Fonseca. The year I was underground Carlos Fonseca was in the library of the Ramírez Goyena school. In the most forthright and brotherly way he said he was no longer a member of UNAP, no longer read Maritain, but had gone on to more advanced positions and to read other sorts of things. That was the last serious conversation we had. Later we went different ways in our political struggles.

UNAP went on. The anti-Somoza opposition united in what was called the Front to Defend the Republic, and UNAP was one of the most instrumental groups in bringing the Front together. The Front was very successful in organizing mass demonstrations. But we were just beginning when Rigoberto López Pérez killed the old Somoza. That was in 1956. The night he shot the dictator Somoza point-blank at a party, three thousand opposition leaders in Nicaragua were immediately rounded up. That would be like taking ten thousand in one night now. They came looking for me in my house in the early morning. They took me away in pajamas, and I was in jail in pajamas for a long time, and no one in my family knew where I was. I was in jail with Pedro Joaquín Chamorro, in the same cell. We were tortured savagely. Pedro Joaquín Chamorro's book *Estirpe Sangrienta* described all our experiences in jail.

I was in prison for only two and a half months. They let me out because the prosecutor of the military court thought I could serve as a witness against Pedro Joaquín. They set me free and they called me to the military court. When I arrived, the prosecutor drew me aside and said, "OK, I worked to get you out so you could say such-and-such."

I answered, "I can't declare that."

"But you're putting me on the spot."

"That's your problem, I'm not going to swear to that." They took me to give testimony, and of course I didn't give testimony against Pedro Joaquín. And then I was free. They were obsessed with passing a sentence on Pedro Joaquín Chamorro because of his paper *La Prensa* and also on the others they had in prison because they assumed they were connected with the small group that took part in the tyrannicide.

After I got out, we analyzed UNAP. We recognized that with a position like ours it was very difficult to get through to the masses. And since the Conservative Party at that time had a strong anti-Somoza position and a strong hold on the people it seemed like a good strategy to get into it in order to influence this great mass of the people and turn it into a party that would be of the people, democratic and revolutionary, and inspired by Christianity. That was why we joined the party.

After the victory of the Cuban Revolution, which had an impact on all the peoples of Latin America and sparked the imagination of young people, we began to think of setting up our own guerrilla forces in Nicaragua. I went to Costa Rica and made contact with Pedro Joaquín Chamorro, who was thinking along the same lines.

By this time, we had put together another opposition coalition called UNO, National Opposition Union. UNO proposed an armed movement against Somoza. When I was in Costa Rica on a ranch belonging to Figueres [hero of the 1948 war, leader of the Liberation Party and president of Costa Rica from 1953 to 1958 and from 1970 to 1974] a delegation came from Fidel Castro to visit Figueres and invite him to Cuba, since there was going to be a large public ceremony and demonstration—this was soon after the victory of the revolution. I jumped at the chance and went with Figueres on the plane Fidel Castro had sent. Pedro Joaquín Chamorro and other opposition leaders followed on a commercial flight.*

We came back to Costa Rica and carried out the action known as *Olama y*

---

*At this point in a long passage, Tefel describes meetings with Castro and Che Guevara. When Tefel asked for support, Guevara said he was committed to a group of Nicaraguan exiles in Havana and so could not help them.—TRANS.

Mollejones. We set out from a place in Costa Rica called La Llorona by plane. We landed in Chontales, but the internal front failed us. The internal front was going to blow up bridges. They were going to do a lot of things, but they didn't do them, and we were left stranded in the hills. Somoza's battalions, about 900 highly trained men at that time, the elite of the Guard, surrounded us. They took us prisoner and put us in jail. Pedro Joaquín Chamorro and I were there more than a year. Then there was an amnesty because of a lot of pressure to set us free both from inside the country and internationally. The Somozas were skillful politicians, quite flexible. They were always tightening up and then loosening things. They would get a tight grip, and then when they had gotten everything under control, let things loose again. When the tide went against them they would go back to killing, torturing, and jailing, and when once again things were under control they would loosen up. That's how they could stay in power for so long, with this loosening and tightening. In all this they got advice and support from the United States.

> **In looking for a revolutionary platform we began with a work toward change that was expressly Christian.**

We were arrested in 1959 and got out in June 1960. While I was in jail there was a convention of the Conservative Party and they elected Agüero president and me secretary. When I got out, I found myself in ideological conflict with Agüero. I challenged him when he was at the height of his popularity. Within the party I began to oppose him ideologically because he wasn't really following a revolutionary line but was an opportunist. Many people criticized me for opposing him, but they recognized that I was right years later when Agüero made a deal with Somoza. Along with a group of young people, I left the Conservative Party and joined the Social Christian Party (PSC) and struggled for several years within it.

What I was always looking for was a structure that would be really revolutionary and could bring about deep change in our country's structures. I didn't find it in the Social Christian Party. So I also left the PSC and threw my energies into INPRHU (Institute for Human Development).

INPRHU was really an agent of change in the country that served as a logistical as well as a financial and ideological support for mass organizations. In it we carried out a work that was deeply and expressly Christian but not sectarian. We helped all kinds of popular organizations get started, from producers cooperatives to labor-union kinds of organizations. Toward the end we were able to set up a front of all the mass organizations existing at that time.

By the time we celebrated INPRHU's tenth anniversary, my position was completely revolutionary. In my tenth anniversary speech I said INPRHU was a great convergence of Christianity, socialism, and nationalistic democracy. Then Pedro Joaquín Chamorro was murdered. I should say that before the murder of Pedro Joaquín we had tried to form a Democratic Socialist Movement. We were meeting here in my house for a year, every Monday. Perhaps we sinned by being intellectuals, although we said we were going to avoid that. We spend a lot of time working things out intellectually and never got involved in the struggle. What we had in mind was a democratic revolutionary movement that would use Marxism as an intellectual tool for interpreting reality. So there were big discussions. Several of this group joined the Sandinista Front. All of us who belonged to that group are in the revolution today.

—In this story, which sheds light on so many things, the Sandinista Front appears only at the end, even though its members had been struggling against Somoza for years. And you've said that you and Carlos Fonseca parted ways politically in your form of struggle if not deep down. How did you see the FSLN's struggle throughout this whole period?

—Frankly, during their first stage I saw it as a movement with very good intentions made up of Nicaraguans who were really patriotic, really revolutionary, but because of their strategy I didn't think they would be able to defeat the dictatorship and imperialism in the medium run. And now that I think about it, I can see that I was right to some degree, because their strategy of prolonged war was not the most apt for winning in Nicaragua. The Sandinista Front won when they took up the insurrectionary proposal in what was a synthesis of the three tendencies. [Tefel is here referring to a three-way split in the Sandinista Front that took place in the mid-1970s and reflected different ideas of strategy: prolonged people's war (peasant war in the hills), proletarian (working with the proletariat, e.g., plantation labor force), insurrectionary (those who believed that the time was becoming ripe for a mass uprising and who favored closer ties with business and middle-class groups).—TRANS.].

I held the insurrectionary thesis and so when I entered into contact with the insurrectionary tendency I began to work with the Sandinista Front. When Somoza's people killed Pedro Joaquín Chamorro I joined UDEL (Democratic Union for Liberation) because at that point it seemed to be the spearhead of the people in their struggle against Somoza. When I joined I was made technical secretary. I thought that what would destroy the Somoza dictatorship and create a new Nicaragua would be the convergence of UDEL, this movement we were trying to form, and the Sandinista Front. That was my intuition. So I began to work in the barrios of Managua, setting up popular organizations to challenge Somoza. That's how I took part in the first strike and in the second one. By that time I was identified with the Sandinista Front.

I think it's important to emphasize that despite what I've said about prolonged war, it was the long and heroic history of the FSLN that made the insurrectionary strategy and the revolutionary victory possible. Without so many years of sacrifice and complete commitment to the struggle, of action and reflection, there would have been no July 19, 1979, which brought complete defeat for Somoza and his genocidal Guard, and the complete victory for the Nicaragua people. It was precisely the convergence of the three strategies that had appeared within the FSLN and the involvement of the masses of the people and of all social sectors in the country in the struggle that forged the revolutionary victory of the people of Sandino. That's why I should recognize that, although in a way I was right in my critique of the prolonged war strategy, I was wrong in not having recognized the historic impact that the long and historic struggle for our liberation would have. And that is due to the remarkable intuition of Carlos Fonseca and his cofounders and to their stubborn perseverance to the point of death.

I have no hesitation in stating that Christianity has a greater influence on this revolution than Marxism-Leninism. It is a great error to ignore that, an error made by some Catholics and some bishops.

—To what extent has your experience of struggle been a Christian experience for you? What role has your faith played? What influences have there been between your political struggle and your Christian faith?

—For me all my activity of political struggle has been demanded by my Christian conscience. There's never been any dichotomy between my political involvement and my Christian involvement. I've never considered politics a religion but a duty in Christian conscience.

—And you've not had any conflicts of conscience or doubts at certain moments in your struggle? Your Christian faith hasn't put any limits on your political struggle?

—No. Speaking of my own experience, and not in the abstract, I have to say no. Not even when I had to deal with the tyrannicide did I feel any limitation, since there was a legitimation for tyrannicide in traditional and orthodox Catholic doctrine. I've never felt that Christianity imposed any limits on my political activity. Quite the contrary. What I've felt is inspiration and support.

—How do you answer those who say that you Christians in the Sandinista state are baptizing a regime that is Marxist-Leninist, totalitarian, and moving toward atheism?

—Well, Lebret used to say that Marx would have to be baptized just as St. Thomas baptized Aristotle. Look, even if what some people say were true, that this is a Marxist-Leninist revolution, Christians would always still have a task to perform in it: to evangelize. The primary thing in the church's mission will always be to evangelize, not to condemn. But I who am a Christian and an active member of the church see that this revolution is not really atheistic and totalitarian, as some say it is. As I see it, they're acting out of their own self-interest, and they're being unfair when they muddy things up and misrepresent the essence of this revolution.

It's true that there are some people who don't formally believe in God. But in what country that sees itself as pluralistic is that not the case? In Nicaragua there are very few unbelievers in comparison to the whole population. There are some cadres who out of dogmatism have a tendency we could call totalitarian. But those people aren't the revolution, they aren't the majority in the revolution, nor do they represent any average in the revolution. Why don't the detractors focus on all the Christian cadres in the revolution? I don't think there's any government in the world that has as many militant Christians as this revolution. Not a one, not a single government in the whole world. Some people want these Christians to leave the government just so they can say that this government is atheistic and so they can turn the world against it. What they don't want is structural change.

I do not hesitate to say that while Marxism has its influence and its role in this revolution, Christianity has more influence than Marxism-Leninism. The grave error of some Catholics and members of the hierarchy is that they ignore that. I believe what Carlos Fonseca used to say, that what had to be formed was a revolutionary national ideology, and that is precisely the synthesis of the three main aspects of our Sandinista people's revolution: Christianity, Marxism, and nationalistic democracy.

—*How far do you think Christianity and Marxism are compatible?*

Some years ago I had my reservations and fears about Marxist materialism. That was to be expected given my formation. Now I see clearly that what Monsignor Arias Caldera said at the inauguration of our People's Eye Clinic is true. He quoted the Belgian theologian Schillebeeckx, saying that a person who doesn't acknowledge God, if he or she loves the people, if he or she loves the poor and struggles for the liberation of the poor with real love, that person is in Christ and is a Christian in some way. That was already in Maritain's book on atheists. It is also in line with the traditional theology we were taught in school. Didn't they tell us that a pagan who didn't recognize God but who led a good life, one that was upright and just, was saved as surely as if he or she had been baptized, by baptism of desire.

> **To me it seems immoral that some Catholics and members of the hierarchy refuse to evangelize the revolution and want it to be antihuman and anti-Christian so they can rend their garments.**

It seems to me that besides our problems with imperialism and the counter-revolution, we are threatened because one sector of the church has taken a position that seems to run against the very interests of Catholicism. Institutionally we can see that normally the Vatican's policy has been to get into governments instead of breaking ties with them, but here the hierarchical church is doing exactly the opposite. Why is it that the policy of the hierarchy, or part of it, the policy of some of the clergy and of some Catholics is leading toward a break? That policy is anti-Christian and immoral. Why, instead of penetrating the revolution to make it more humanistic, more and more democratic, more and more inspired by Christianity, are they trying to do the exact opposite? Why are they trying to make it as antidemocratic as possible, as antihuman as possible, as anti-Christian as possible, so they can then shout and rend their garments?

It is my desire and hope that above everything else what will prevail and be strengthened and be evident will be the moral reserves of the Sandinista revolution, which are deeply rooted in the people, are democratic, and are inspired by Christianity. I have great hopes that this revolution can become more and more human, democratic, and socialist. I don't think there is any contradiction between socialism, democracy, and humanism. I believe democracy doesn't reach its fulness except within socialism, humanism doesn't reach its fulness except within socialism. And I believe socialism doesn't become authentic and deeply socialist unless it is humanistic and democratic.

—*So is the great challenge of the Nicaraguan revolution that of bringing about the synthesis that hasn't occurred yet in processes in history, either in the existing democracies or in existing socialisms?*

—Exactly. Without falling into anti-Sovietism, which is the other ideological armor for the interests of capitalism and imperialism, and maintaining a deep respect for other revolutions, especially the Cuban Revolution, which has been the pioneer in the liberation of Latin America and a pioneer of solidarity with our revolution and our people, that is our great challenge in history: to bring about that synthesis and create a new Latin American model of socialism, one that can serve as an inspiration (not for copying) for the rest of the peoples of Latin America and the Third World.

But all the enemies of fully democratic and authentic socialism—reactionaries and imperialists on one side and dogmatists on the other—and a part of the church as well, they all want to keep the Sandinista people's revolution from moving along that road. They don't want to see that synthesis of democracy and socialism achieved.

As I finish editing this interview, I look over the minister's writings, and I see this aspiration expressed both before and after the revolutionary victory:

1972: "We may ask ourselves whether we Latin Americans are going to find our own route toward overcoming marginality, underdevelopment, and social injustice, and toward freeing ourselves from dependence. Will we be able to find our way in the revolutionary process of change and development, creating a spirit and ethos that is communitarian, austere, brotherly/sisterly, involving the people in the work of the nation, institutionalizing people's participation in the centers of power, guaranteeing that freedom which is essential to human beings while at the same time structuring a system that is effective and dynamic in the realms of politics and economics?" (from the epilogue to Tefel's book *El Infierno de los Pobres*).

1979: "The fact that the Sandinista revolution is Nicaraguan and grew out of Nicaraguan conditions gives it the option of forging a socialist democracy, which will constitute a new model of development and social progress. I say this because in the world there are countries that are democratic, very democratic, but not as socialist as Nicaragua must be in order to reach the humanistic fulness of complete development. On the other hand there are countries that are socialist, very socialist, but not democratic as Nicaragua must be, after forty-five years of dictatorship, in order to build up the New Homeland of free people" (from Tefel's essay "The Sandinista Revolution").

In his introduction to that essay Reinaldo Antonio Tefel wrote this phrase in capital letters: "NEITHER ANOTHER CUBA, NOR ANOTHER PUERTO RICO, BUT A NEW NICARAGUA!"

7

CÉSAR DELGADILLO
and TERESA CARDENAL

General Director of the National Administration
of Ports

"In this revolution we are better able to practice Christianity"

César Delgadillo was born in Corinto on October 29, 1932. He studied
international and consular law. From 1969 to 1979 he worked in customs,
transportation, ports, and imports/exports with local and foreign companies.

He was one of the founders of the Social Christian Party (PPSC) and an active member from 1959 onwards. Teresa and César were married in 1954, and have seven children and five grandchildren. Teresa Cardenal was born in Granada on August 18, 1934. A clothing designer and housewife, she was a founding member of AMPRONAC, the Association of Nicaraguan Women.

●

It seemed like a good idea to interview a married couple together, a Christian man and woman who are active revolutionaries. The idea would be to discuss their individual daily lives and their relationship as spouses and as parents to see to what extent each acted separately and to what extent they coordinated their criteria and their activities in their twofold militancy, revolutionary and Christian.

So here before me are César Delgadillo and Tere Cardenal. Their seventeen-year-old son Alvaro, their sixth child, has brought me to the house in the family car. It was pleasant to get out of Managua in the calm, cool air of an early Sunday morning. César and Tere live in Esquipulas on Kilometer 13 of the highway to Masaya, quite close to the Santiago volcano. In an open and bright parlor downstairs, the three of us relax and chat early this Sunday morning.

●

Q—How did you meet? When did you get married?

Tere answers immediately: We met outside Nicaragua. We were both studying in the United States and we went to a party with some Latin Americans. That's where we met. And, well, we fell in love. That was more than thirty years ago.

César: In 1951.

Tere goes on: We were engaged for three years. It was hard, because he moved to Philadelphia and I stayed in Washington. We got together from time to time and we wrote. And when we both finished our studies we came here to Nicaragua and got married. That was almost thirty years ago. We have seven children and five grandchildren. There were six, but one died last year. We're expecting two more grandchildren this year.

My family seemed to be very Christian, but when the revolution took place, most of them left the country.

—What impact has the revolution had in your family relations on both sides and in your own family?

César begins: On the Delgadillo side, my family is small. On my mother's side, the Machado side, it's a little bigger. Many members of the Machado family are outside the country, some because they were part of the government structure in the past. They say I was one of the few anti-Somocistas and revolutionaries in the Machado family. There are very few Machados in the country who are part of the revolutionary process. On the Delgadillo side, since it's a smaller family, fewer have left. My brother and I are part of the process. He lives in Costa Rica, but he works in a shipping company that's part of the Nicaraguan government. Some of my uncles are with the process, but not so directly as my brother and I. Other members of the family have stayed here, even though their children have left.

—In my family, *adds Tere*, there's been a real falling apart. First, there are a lot of us, thirteen brothers and sisters. The funny part of it is that my family, the Cardenals, has always stood out as a very Christian family. Everything my father did was directed by Jesuits. He was a great admirer of the Jesuits and had all of us educated according to the rules and regulations of the church—Catholic schools, Catholic university, and always with the Jesuits. He himself made the Spiritual Exercises every year. He was a good man, and everyone loved and respected him. That gives you an idea of the Christian atmosphere in our home.

But when the revolution came along we realized that everyone understood this Christianity differently. For me the most important thing is love, to love your neighbor. What I see is that this revolution favors serving your neighbor. It demands sacrifices, it demands overcoming your selfishness, and sacrificing lots of things. The few of us who have had everything at our disposal must sacrifice whatever needs to be sacrificed in order that the poor majority of the people may have a decent life, a human life. When this demand became clear, what happened? The family—my brothers' and sisters' children, whom we used to see all the time, since we were a very close family—the family has completely fallen apart. Almost all of them have left. Some for Guatemala, some for the United States, others for Costa Rica. All of them looking for a better life economically, since they say you can't live with the salary limit here in Nicaragua. They don't put the education they've had in the United States to work for the people here. They go to other countries and put that education to work just to serve themselves, so they can live better.

In our own family unit, we and our children, we're quite united. We're happy since we all speak the same language and we're all involved in the same thing. But that's not how it is with my brothers and sisters. That makes it hard to communicate, since we have ideas and positions that are very different. But I still don't want to break off from them. They're my brothers and sisters and I love them. Anyway I think I can always do something, at least communicate my happiness. I'm a happy woman, quite content. I, who'd never worked before, since my husband was well paid and there was no need for me to work, now I'm working. I help with our family income, since salaries in the revolutionary government are lower than in the private sector. Our revolution can't give us all we might need. It can't, given the conditions, both internal and external. So there are a lot of things we have to make up, even though we've accepted a lower standard of living. But we're happy and all our children are quite satisfied with these sacrifices. They're all working and studying.

—*One of your brothers who did stay behind, Tere, is quite visible in the ideological struggle against the people's revolution as an advisor and writer for* La Prensa, *which is clearly opposed to the way the Sandinistas are leading the revolution and to those who support it. Without doubting your affection as brother and sister, I'd like to know how you explain his position, which is so opposed to yours.*

—I wouldn't want to judge him. It seems to me that he got used to living as part of a privileged elite and it's very hard to leave that. Then there's the fear that this revolution could become Marxist-Leninist, atheistic, and that it could restrict freedom. I've heard him speak of losing the freedom to act. I also think the environment he lives in has its impact. Really, though, I don't understand how this brother of mine and I could go in such opposite directions, given how much we've loved each other. We got along very well until the revolutionary victory, and then everything changed.

César chimes in: I think one of the decisive factors could have been the mental structure coming from the capitalist education he had, which influences the way he sees things. Frankly, we have to recognize that the revolution has frustrated aspirations to grab more and more, since it's inconceivable that in this country you should be able to grab things for your own selfish use. The revolution has frustrated the middle class's aspirations to rise up to the level of the plutocracy, to the bourgeoisie, to the big money. Since these possibilities have been cut off, the reactionary forces in Nicaragua solidified in these two social structures: those who left because they were fully identified with the Somoza structures, and those who stayed, who weren't directly connected to the Somoza structures but were connected to the capitalist structure.

I sum it up like this: this revolution has had two stages. One was our struggle to wipe out the Somoza dictatorship, to throw off the yoke, the exploitation. The second stage is the head-on struggle with capitalism. And the third will be the building of the new society. That's how I visualize our process.

> **The revolution opens space for a life that is honest, sincere, and Christian.**

—*You have publicly declared your Christian belief and practice your Christianity in the midst of this process. What kind of Christianity is that? How did it begin, how has it grown, and how have you related it to the struggles that have taken place?*

César begins, pausing frequently: In our family Christianity was not inspired by the conviction of a faith steeped in the gospel and committed to putting it into practice. The impulse of our Christianity was transmitted from generation to generation by tradition, and meant mainly going to Mass and knowing an adhoc catechism with very little theology. This Christianity affected me in the sense that it kept alive a certain Christian tradition, rather spiritualistic and tied to folk customs.

I think I've found the most solid and genuine aspect of Christianity by coming to understand the struggle of peasants and workers. I was born in Corinto, Nicaragua's main port. There I saw workers exploited, neglected. I first stood against management a long time ago in one of the workers' struggles for their rights. That was in the 1960s, when I was working in the government of René Schick and the military was sent to Corinto to smash the workers. I was one of those who opposed that. The government then blacklisted workers whom they categorized as "communists," or those who were putting foreign ideas into the labor movement. The labor movement in Corinto has carried on one of this country's greatest struggles. One reason was that the workers had contact with ships from around the world, and could talk to many foreigners.

Years later in a Cursillo de Cristiandad I publicly confessed that I had been part of that exploitation, that oppression, squeezing the juice from the worker for my own selfish benefit. But on that occasion when I opposed what the government was doing, they took me away from the bargaining table, since they saw I was against management. They all thought I should be against the workers since I was on the management commission.

This experience helped to equip me for deeper involvement in the struggle. I got to know many revolutionary people, particularly people who were already part of the structure of the Sandinista Front. For example, Manolo Morales Peralta, a man who struggled against exploitation, a man of sacrifice. Together with him we helped the Sandinista Front. We became more wholeheartedly involved, so that in 1970, along with Manolo, I had a hand in helping Carlos Fonseca, Humberto Ortega, and others get out of jail in Costa Rica. We helped Carlos Fonseca's wife, Haydee Terán de Fonseca, with money and transporting some weapons. It all worked out well, and it was one of the things that made it possible for Carlos Fonseca to continue working in the revolutionary process.

There was a time when I insisted that we had to exhaust all legal means before going into armed struggle. In 1972, before the earthquake, I went to a meeting in Granada where there were quite a few people from the Sandinista Front. We agreed that the structures for legal struggle were not effective, were not allowed to work in our country, and in fact, had been exhausted. In 1970 we had collected a long list of signatures on a petition against the government. The government showed its aloofness and disdain by responding with a farce. [Delgadillo is presumably referring to the 1972 "pact" Somoza arranged with his nominal opposition, bypassing genuine elections by setting up a triumvirate including himself and a constituent assembly, an arrangement he unilaterally terminated after the December 1972 earthquake.—TRANS.] In that meeting we agreed to keep taking part in legal struggles, but at the same time armed struggle would begin. That was the point at which we consciously became involved in armed struggle. One decisive event was the split in the Nicaraguan Social Christian Party, the party of the Christian Democrats. The Popular Social Christian Party was set up, and it accepted the need for armed struggle against the existing structures of oppression so as to create a new society.

I believe that in this struggle we have been putting the old person to death and giving birth to the new person. I still have my bad habits and faults, but we are in daily training to shape up. For me, one of the basic accomplishments of the revolution has been to give me and others a chance to live an honest, sincere, and Christian life.

My husband started my conversion to true Christianity, by teaching me justice and detachment.

Tere speaks up: My case is different. I didn't really go along with César at first. He began my conversion. I used to say to him, "How come you're involved in the opposition. You're going to lose your job." I'd say things like that, know what I mean? But with his way of arguing, he slowly taught me detachment and gradually awakened in me a yearning for justice. It was he who began this change in me. Then came the Cursillo de Cristiandad where we became even more concerned—or at least I did. We formed a group of people who were concerned and who weren't satisfied with the cursillo (its practices, its paternalism, its "charity" toward the neighbor) and were looking for something deeper. By now we were looking for a change in structures.

At that point we formed a group to meet every week, and we studied what capitalism and socialism meant. A whole new panorama opened up, and I came to understand everything my husband, César, had been trying to tell me from the start. I had the same concerns, but it wasn't easy to find an outlet for them. Then my moment came with the drawing up of a list of people who might work together to organize women.

A whole bunch of us women got together, almost all upper class. It began as an organization to defend human rights. When they said what it was all about, people began to say, "Well, I have to go home and check with my husband to see what he thinks." "I can't make a decision here without consulting with my husband." All those who had been invited were backing off. My turn came: "What about you, Tere, what do you think?"

"Well, look," I said, "I think César and I know each other well enough, I know how he thinks and he knows how I think, so I don't have to check with him. I'll say yes right now."

"And would you be willing to be part of the national executive board?"

"Yes, I would."

So the next one said, "Me too," and so it went, and we got the group started. It's a great honor for me to say that I was a founding member of AMPRONAC (Women's Association to Deal with National Problems).

> I will be relentlessly opposed to the revolution if I see that it does not benefit the poor majority.

—You claim that, precisely as Christians, you are revolutionaries. The revolution is a sociopolitical project. And the Christian faith is a living bond with the God of Jesus Christ, who lives in the church, personally and in community. What sort of convergences do you see between your Christian faith and the project of the Sandinista people's revolution?

César responds: In a political talk I once said that providing housing, giving people food, increasing production, are things that Christianity proposes for me in biblical terms, and that I find no difficulty in collaborating in this kind of thing with someone I know is a Marxist-Leninist if that person respects my Christian faith as I respect his or her Marxism-Leninism. I'd go further. If that person's economic vision is in accordance with the goals we've set for advancing the country, I have nothing against concretely helping to set up an economic system as viewed from a Marxist perspective, as long as it is benefiting the whole population, the vast majority. I could hold back from collaborating only if that Marxist-Leninist were to tell me that I must not believe in anything beyond because it doesn't bring any benefit. Those are personal matters of conscience that I cannot give up. That person should not intrude on my faith, just as I don't intrude on their "belief," as some people put it. The Marxist-Leninist may believe that everything takes place here; we Christians believe there is a beyond.

Tere steps in: All you have to do is ask: what does the revolution aim to do? Who is it going to benefit? Sure, we were used to the previous structures. Then the only ones who benefited were a small group, a tiny group, no one else. And that's why this small group is unhappy; they see that they're no longer in charge, that they're no longer important.

I remember when they put my son César in jail. It was the same day the UN office of Managua was occupied. I took part in a demonstration there. One of the tear gas bombs they threw at us—I picked it up and threw it back at the

Guardia. I was afraid because it came out on TV and I was afraid Alesio Gutiérrez, who was part of the repressive apparatus, would notice that, and it would affect my son, who had been jailed that day. Well, the next day I disguised my appearance. I went to a beauty parlor, got all made up, quite elegantly, purse, high heels and all, to go talk to Alesio Gutiérrez. He treated me well, and I paid my fine—he wouldn't take a check, of course, since that would leave a record—and I got my son out. In other words, you had privileges with anyone in the Guardia. If you looked well-dressed, as if you belonged to the upper class, they treated you differently.

Now all that is gone, and the people who no longer have that power, those who used to enjoy privileges with those who were ruling before, must resent it. Besides, they can't bear the change the revolution means for their lives, since they can't go to Europe every year any more, they can't keep their beach house, and they can't keep a chauffeur and a lot of maids. The only avenue for their protest is religion, so that's what they latch onto, in order to try to recover the power that would enable them to get their privileges back. They manipulate religion as a bulwark against the revolution. Bourgeois religion. But if you dig down into this revolution, you will find that there's not a single law that has been made that is not to benefit the people. Therefore, it is benefiting the people of God. There's not a single change that the revolution has made that goes against the gospel. With its changes, the revolution is making it easier for us to live the true Christianity of the gospel.

César speaks up: I don't see that the revolutionary process intends to attack or eliminate the Nicaraguan people's Christian faith. In fact, I see it favoring the faith by the laws it is laying down, by rebuilding and developing the country, by the very process we are living.

Tere says: The Nicaraguan people are Christian and they will not stop being Christian. If the revolution continues to work on behalf of the majority of the people, they will support it and at the same time continue to be Christians.

This downstairs part of the house has a flavor of Spain in the windows with the ornamental iron, but the plants are tropical. Cool air comes in through the open window. The truck has come by twice spraying water on the dusty streets.

We have to pass again, as we leave, through the town. I look at the poverty of the dirt streets and the shacks of the workers and peasants who make up the majority of the three thousand inhabitants of Esquipulas.

8

RICARDO E. CHAVARRÍA

Vice-Minister of the Nicaraguan Energy Institute

**"I'm now serving my people as a militant Christian
and as a revolutionary"**

*Ricardo E. Chavarría was born in Diriamba, Carazo, April 15, 1944. At 18
he entered a seminary for late vocations in Antioquia, Colombia. He studied
theology in Salamanca (Spain) and at the Gregorian University in Rome. In
1970 he was ordained in Managua and served there as a priest for five years. He*

was involved in the anti-Somoza activities of the Christian communities. In 1976 he left the priesthood and went to the United States to study sociology at Ohio University and at Tulane University in New Orleans. Upon receiving his dispensation from Rome, he married Milagros Lanza Morales. They have two children. In 1982, Chavarría was made Vice-Minister of the Nicaraguan Energy Institute (INE).

●

I had been told that Ricardo Chavarría had been a priest, and a popular one, that seven years ago he had left the priesthood, and that the Managua priests who had been his colleagues remembered him fondly and held him in esteem.

I was acquainted with Milagros, his wife. I had said hello to Ricardo a few times, had seen him in church-related meetings, and had read articles of his on the church in the revolutionary process and on the problems of Christians who were involved in that process. At that time he seemed to me to be a layperson with a good formation, conversant with theology, but it didn't occur to me that he might have been a priest.

One night I had supper with Ricardo and Milagros in their house on the outskirts of Managua. Their little son, Daniel, was there, dark-faced like his father, serious, lively, fond of drawing.

In addition to Ricardo's position and his active role as a Christian layperson, I was intrigued by the reputation he had had as a priest. I asked for an interview and he gave it to me in his office at INE. That same night Milagros felt the first contractions announcing the arrival of their second child, María-Gabriela.

We are striving to achieve energy independence for the country.

Chavarría—A good deal of the future of our country's economic and social development depends on INE. The problem is to assure the country the energy resources it needs for development. In my position as INE Vice-Minister I am involved in labor relations. INE has over four thousand workers. "Labor relations" has many facets and deals with the expectations of different social groups. The idea is to mesh everybody's expectations, relating them in a way that is minimally conflictive, in an educational process set within the framework of our revolution.

Q—Tell me something about INE during Somoza's time. How was it then? How has it changed with the revolution?

—In Somoza's time it was called ENALUF (National Light and Power

Company) and only produced electric energy, operating electric plants and distributing and selling electric energy. ENALUF contracted with foreign companies to design and build new projects and sold electric energy to private companies, or so-called cooperatives, which sold energy they had not produced, adding to the cost. As a result the people were exploited. That's what ENALUF was all about.

The revolution changed the ministry's objectives and broadened its role. The private companies were nationalized and the cooperatives were brought into a single system. ENALUF became the institution charged with directing the whole question of energy in all its forms and dimensions.

Starting this year, 1983, we will be generating electric energy from steam in the geothermic field of the Momtombo volcano. We face the challenge of developing thirteen hydroelectric projects by the year 2000. Feasibility studies for other energy areas, such as biomass, are underway.

At present our economy is tremendously dependent on petroleum we don't have, so dependent in fact that almost 60 percent of the proceeds from our exports go to pay for the petroleum we consume. That means almost all our coffee and a good deal of our cotton goes to pay for petroleum.

—Let's go into what motivates you personally in your professional work. I'd like to know about whatever revolutionary kinds of motivation you have for serving the people, and even more, whether you are motivated by Christian faith and at what level.

—I'm a sociologist. I was with my wife in the United States when our first child was born and the Sandinista People's Revolution was victorious. One thing became quite clear to us: we had to come back to Nicaragua to work and serve the people in their revolutionary process. We returned in mid-1980 after spending almost five years studying outside. I never thought I would have the kind of professional position I have within the revolution. My only thought was that we were going to come to work and serve. Presumably, I was coming to teach in the university. I could have gone into some other agency just as well as into this one. If we weren't in a revolution, the normal thing would be for me to be a professor in the university. But the fact that we are in a revolution has enabled us to take on a flexible attitude, in the sense of being available to serve the process wherever we're needed, without being concerned about personal or family interests and advantages.

I agreed to work here in INE because it seemed like a good way to serve the cause of the people in the revolution. The very day I began I had to make decisions. I sometimes made mistakes during those early days. Two years later they asked me to work at a different level, with more responsibility, and here I am. The government junta appointed me as one of the Vice-Ministers in this agency.

Milagros and I took all this on, looking at it both as the reality we are living and as grace, as a reality that is gratuitous. And we've taken it with gratitude, in a spirit of service; we want to respond with joy, with dedication, trying to do our utmost. We're quite aware that we have numerous faults but we're striving to keep educating ourselves in this process.

I stopped being a priest, but I didn't stop being a Christian and an active member of the church.

—I'm a believer and a militant Christian. I'm a Catholic. Eight years ago, I was a priest. I was a priest and carried out a pastoral ministry in Managua for five years. I stopped being a priest, but I didn't stop being a believer and an active member of the Catholic Church.

—*I was aware of this journey in your faith. I've been interested in interviewing you in order to come to know the experience of faith of a Vice-Minister in the revolution, one who was a priest and who continues to regard himself as a Catholic while holding this job in a revolutionary state. When and why did you leave the priesthood?—unless that's something too sensitive to talk about.*

—No, not at all. I have no problem talking about it since I took those steps with discernment of spirit and it's all been integrated into my life in a positive way.

I left the priesthood on January 10, 1976, the day I presided over the Eucharist for the last time. Since that day I've felt very much at peace and experienced a great deal of freedom. That was a very strange day with a good deal of happiness and at the same time a lot of sadness. I was ordained a priest on October 24, 1970, so I carried out a priestly ministry for five years.

Why did I leave the priesthood? My experience in the priestly ministry was quite fruitful in the sense that I was accepted in my communities and was responsive to them. Nevertheless, that total dedication to priestly ministry didn't provide me with a complete answer to my decision to be celibate. I had made that decision quite honestly, believing that dedication to pastoral ministry would fill my life. In fact, I didn't see those priests who weren't wholeheartedly involved in a pastoral mission (as I understood it) as very priestly. Some were educators or teachers or were involved in social activities, while I regarded the priesthood as meaning complete dedication to pastoral work with the community of believers, involving evangelization, sacraments, and prayer. In my commitment to priestly ministry, I gradually became aware that I couldn't handle the solitude, as much as I tried to fill it up spiritually. A long time ago I felt in tune with the French priests in El Prado, and I found their evangelical way of life to be a response that was rich in spiritual life. For one reason or another, I lost contact with them. I was very busy pastorally, but I finally had to recognize that even though I was good at my ministry, even though I preached well, even though I was responsive to the people, even though I had good ideas about pastoral planning, and even though the bishop trusted me, I should not continue to be a priest if I could not be really fulfilled alone.

I tried to respond to this deep questioning with the means I thought would be best: a spiritual retreat. That brought me a great deal of peace. I became convinced that I should leave the priesthood, even if it meant I had to give up things that made for security and privilege in the church and in society. That was true. The priest's status was, and still is, a platform for easy security and privileges connected with power and influence, in both our church and our society. In that sense, I was going to slip down and lose a lot of advantages. I would have to face a situation where people would point a finger at me and some would condemn me. It's not easy to undergo that experience and keep your balance. However, the decision brought me peace, and other priests were like brothers, listening to me and standing by me. At the same time, many people were quite surprised. They said it wasn't possible, that they could believe anything except that I should take such a step. But I had made a firm decision, very much following my conscience, on July 31, the feast of St. Ignatius Loyola, in the Tepeyac retreat house in Granada. And from that day on, I felt a great freedom of spirit.

After leaving the priesthood, I got to know Milagros. I had the opportunity for professional training. First, I went to Canada at the end of February 1976 to learn English. We wrote back and forth. After getting the papal dispensation, I came back to Nicaragua. We were married and left for the United States. We are fortunate to see our love realized in a family, and we are growing in our commitment to serve the revolution of our people. That's important for our Christian faith.

I'd like to mention something that influenced my faith a great deal. Before the insurrection, when the Sandinista Front was struggling and suffering underground and I was working as a priest, I was invited to work with the Front. I took part in hunger strikes. I remember spending twenty-two days in a hunger strike with the mothers of political prisoners and so getting a number of our Sandinistas out of jail. Before that, the bishop had told us to leave the churches, since a group of priests had joined Christian student groups in order to offer the witness of our love and to protect them from the barbarism of the Somoza regime. We obeyed the bishop but we didn't give up our solidarity with the cause, so we stayed with the mothers in the Red Cross building. I also took part in student strikes. For me there was no alternative. Not to have done that would have been a betrayal—betrayal of the people, of my community, of my faith, and of my priesthood, which all put me at the service of the people, and especially of those who were suffering the most. Just as in other circumstances it would have been a betrayal not to respond to some unexpected call, so it would be a betrayal now not to say "Yes" when I am entrusted with some responsibility that calls for service.

In my work within the revolution, I try to live the faith with the spirituality of the presence of God.

*—You left the priesthood, but the experience of priestly ministry is an
integral part of your life and your faith. In your work and in your life today
how do you integrate Christian identity and political and revolutionary identity?*

—I believe the Lord has given me the grace not to emphasize that distinction
to the point of separating or dividing those two identities. I live them together.
Here where I work, the people around me and the workers in general know I
was a priest and sometimes they still call me "Father." Since there are priests
who are government ministers in the revolution, some people think I'm also a
priest. It's funny, but in a way, I sometimes believe I'm still exercising the
ministry. Really. That's what I experience. But it is a lay ministry, completely
lay.

*—You've spoken of two dimensions of your Christian faith in the revolu-
tion. One reaches out, having to do with your relationships with your coworkers, and another is internal and personal, the experience of the presence of God
in events and the spirituality of exercising power. I'm going to ask you about a
third dimension involved in Christian identity, the ecclesial aspect. Do you
publicly live and express your membership in the church?*

—Yes. First, there are plenty of occasions to express my membership in the
church in the work, even through public statements. It comes up in relations
with others and in meetings. But the place where it happens explicitly for me is
in the community of Christians in the Revolution. Our community is a group
of Christians who are sharing a similar experience, since we are all actively
committed to the revolution. Most of us work in the government, and our
experience of Christian life goes back a number of years. Some have been
involved for twenty or twenty-five years, through cursillos, the charismatic
movement, the Christian Family Movement, or grassroots Christian communities.

In my case, I was a priest and participated in the formation of grassroots
Christian communities. Now that I am a layman, and working within the
process of the revolution, I share with others all the problems involved in their
striving to be Christians and to be church. Both my wife and I are involved. The
deepest reason for being part of this new Christian community movement is the
need we feel to share, to analyze and deepen, at the level of Christian and
ecclesial faith, our experience of living a new Christian spirituality, one that is
set within our life and work in the process taking place in the people. It is there
that the Lord comes forth to meet us and makes us discover and take on the
Christian values of the gospel with dimensions and perspectives we had never

before suspected. We are living a challenge and a marvelous adventure for Christians and for the church.

> **As Christians we accept voluntary impoverishment so that the condition of the poor majority in Nicaragua can improve.**

—One of the problems in all this is the widening gulf between us and our relatives who don't opt for the revolution as we do. We may even come to a parting of the ways. For us the point is to understand ongoing history through our faith, and to understand the ongoing history of our faith itself, of what we live and experience as Christians.

Another problem area we experience is that of voluntary impoverishment. We are living it as a Christian experience, evangelical poverty, as the enrichment of our faith, as we become poorer by working in a revolutionary process that seeks to better the living conditions of the poor majority through deep changes in our society. Most of our brothers and sisters in the community are people who came from a high position in society, from the upper middle class or even from Nicaragua's aristocratic class. They faced the question of having to leave everything behind, or felt a calling to do so, to lose their profits, and to risk everything so that Nicaragua could really be free and could change its structures toward a society more just and family-like, where goods would be better distributed. A good number of them have gone so far that they now experience a real economic tightening. They no longer get high incomes in their careers and positions. They've handed over their property, those who had some. Others, those of us who didn't have property, like me, we've given up the possibility of having property as we might have otherwise had under other structures. This process of gradual economic impoverishment doesn't make us sad, but is strengthening us in the faith and in the social commitment of faith for the benefit of the poorest.

We are quite aware that we are not poor yet, since we don't really share the social and economic conditions of most of our people. But we are aware that our chances for moving up, for amassing wealth, are gone. In practice, the revolution forces us to give up that possibility. And we have accepted this new situation with the freedom of our Christian faith, and that assures our break with the past, with our old being. At the same time, it places before us the challenge of the ideal that the Christian should face at some moment in his or her life: to leave everything behind and follow Christ in his mission to liberate history. This Christian perspective on impoverishment in solidarity is one of the marks of our community.

The changes going on in the people's process in Nicaragua are connected to what is essential in the Christian church: the preferential option for the poorest. That option is not a whim, it is not an arbitrary decision, it is not something to be left up to the private initiatives of people who have special charisms or to exceptional individuals. It is rather a universal vocation of the church, just as following Jesus Christ, sanctity through following Jesus Christ, is a universal calling of the church. It is as "church" that you make the preferential option for the poor, not through private initiative.

When Ricardo returned the text of the interview after checking it, he attached a handwritten letter, dated January 14, 1983:

Today, a few hours before joining the Omar Torrijos Brigade, I am finishing checking the transcription of the interview. I'll leave it up to your literary judgment how much you think should be changed.

I'll be in combat these next two months. I was chosen for this new mission from among some of the best Sandinista cadres, but I know that in every choice God's loving hand is present. I entrust Milagros and our two children to God's care and to that of my brothers and sisters in the faith. Of you I ask a solidarity that will have its effect before the eyes of the Father, and so your prayer and mine will be joined in the chalice which I drink today with Jesus for the resurrection of our people, for today they have more hope than ever before.

I hope we meet again when I come back. Milagros says she's going to arrange two parties. One will be with our coworkers, and the other will be with those with whom, through faith, we intimately acknowledge the source and destiny of all human history.

> A brotherly embrace in Christ,
> Ricardo

9

VIDALUZ MENESES

General Director of Libraries and Archives

"Three things in my life are inseparable: poetry, my Christian faith, and the revolution"

Vidaluz Meneses was born in Matagalpa on May 28, 1944, and went to school there and in Managua. She has worked in different institutions (such as the Agriculture School in Rivas and the Central American University) and has promoted cultural activities. She was married in 1966 and separated from her husband in 1981. The two share the responsibility for their four children, whose ages range from eight to fifteen. She is General Director of Libraries and Archives and works in the Ministry of Culture. A member of the editorial staff of Ventana, *the weekly popular culture supplement to the FSLN newspaper* Barricada, Vidaluz *is a poet and belongs to the Union of Writers in the Sandinista Association of Cultural Workers. She has published two books of poetry:* Llama Guardada *(1975), and* El Aire Que Me Llama *(1982).*

●

Vidaluz Meneses tells me that her poetry, her faith, and the revolution are inseparable in her life. When Vidaluz says this to me as we begin the interview sitting in the living room of her small house in the Pancasán neighborhood of Managua, I realize that she has fully defined herself to me. My interview must unravel the threads of this woman's life, woven by faith and poetry on the rough loom of the people's struggle.

My poetry is my life. I believe that the word commits us, and that Nicaragua's poets are its prophets.

Q—Why are there so many women poets in Nicaragua? Because they're Nicaraguans or because they're women?

Meneses—Because they're Nicaraguan women. The poet José Coronel Urtecho says: *"Mujer que se desvela, mujer que se rebela."* ("Woman who works day and night, woman who rebels.") We got started on the road to women's liberation by starting to write. Our liberation is characteristically Latin American, integrated into the liberation of the entire people, which means it is both economic and political. We include the liberation of our gender, the liberation of women, but not like some feminist movements in capitalist bourgeois societies.

There is no country in the world with more poets than Nicaragua—men and women. It is as though being born here means being born from the womb of poetry. In Nicaragua poetry gushes forth, spontaneous and deep, like the water in its lakes and the smoke and steam from the mouths of its five active volcanos. Poetry is a way of being Nicaraguan, highly valued by ordinary people.

—Who were your first poets, Vidaluz? your favorites, the ones that always stay with you?

—Joaquín Pasos. It's too bad he died so young, when he was 32. But he produced very good poetry from the time he was 15, and he is one of the great

figures in our literature. At present two poets constitute key reference points, two poets who have created schools: Carlos Martínez Rivas, and Ernesto Cardenal. Cardenal is outgoing, his language is open. Martínez Rivas's poetic language is of a more closed style: he says you have to conceive of poetry like the perfect crime. You feel a pull in two directions: to be accessible to the people—a revolutionary need—and to develop yourself in literary terms.

In Nicaragua poetry was a weapon in the anti-Somoza struggle. It had to be that way. Previously poetry had been a protest against the imperialistic occupation and pillage of the United States, which since 1855 has viewed Nicaragua as an attractive and easy prize. It started when William Walker arrived with his "filibusters," took as much as he wanted, proclaimed himself president of Nicaragua, and was recognized as such by the Pierce administration in the United States. That is why there was a great deal of antiimperialist poetry. From Rubén Darío's "Anti-Ode to Roosevelt," through Joaquín Pasos and Fernando Gordillo, and up to the verses that come out of the People's Poetry Workshops today, denouncing American aggression against the Sandinista revolution.

Vidaluz tells me:

—Nicaragua's poets are its prophets: they denounce injustice or the people's suffering and announce the new society, love, justice, peace.

The guerrilla poets, young poets who died in the struggle, are the greatest prophets and witnesses of the new Nicaragua. The people call them heroes and martyrs.

—Let's hear about your poet-martyrs.

—Leonel Rugama. You can't help but identify with him as a poet and a revolutionary. His Christian roots stayed with him in his poetry even though he became a Marxist. He left the seminary and rebelled against a church that pulled us toward a vision that was alien to our situation and our cause. More than anything else he rebelled against Somoza and they killed him. He fell in battle.

Ricardo Morales Avilés is another great revolutionary and great poet who is dead. They died in combat, absolutely lucid about their role in the struggle, generously giving of themselves. They are our poet-martyrs. Fernando Gordillo is another great poet who died very young. I was a friend of his. They were all remarkable. Leonel Rugama did a portrait of them (and himself) in these wonderful lines: "The heroes didn't say/ they would die for their country;/ they just died."

In Nicaragua in the wake of the revolutionary victory, the number of poets, men and women, from all walks of life, is increasing—peasants, workers, students, members of the army and the police, those who work in the Ministry of the Interior.

More than a hundred Poetry Workshops have created poets all over Nicaragua, and they have produced poems expressing the experiences of these years of revolutionary struggle. The historical memory of the people's liberation is being stored up in verse. Through their remarkable National Literacy Crusade these people are discovering for themselves their own consciousness, their own thinking, their own word, their own Nicaraguan culture, which was stolen from them and kept from them for so long. It is here that the Nicaraguan revolution gets down to its deepest level.

—*How long have you been writing poetry?*

—I began in adolescence. Diaries were very popular among my generation, little notebooks where you used to write all the important things that happened during the day, and you expressed your most intimate and personal thoughts. I can't figure out why, instead of doing it in prose, I began to put everything I felt and thought in verse.

—*Among all the valuable things in your life, where do you place poetry?*

—There are three things in my life that I can't separate: poetry, my Christian life, and then, the revolution. I recognize that these three things in my life flow together into one, into this thirst for something transcendent, something not yet possessed. Many of us believe that the word commits us. And every thought that comes to me from the angle of poetry, inevitably I relate it to Christianity as I've learned it and as I conceive it. Theologians might be scandalized, but I connect the poetic word with that verse that is so profound: "First there was the Word, and the Word became flesh." First comes the word: you put it forth in an instant and out of it you draw what is most personal from deep inside yourself. That word commits you and demands that you follow through. My style is lyric, that is, I write that kind of intimate poetry that gives voice to what is personal. Practically all my poetry is an x-ray of the internal process of my development as a person. In that sense I can say that my poetry is my life.

The writing of poetry is spreading and reaching ordinary people; there are more and more books of poetry coming out. I have seen eleven appear in two years. You can buy the new books in the people's supermarkets, sometimes very cheaply. And there are recitals for the people. Every week is "Poetry Wednesday" and poets get their turn in the huge Rubén Darío theater. Vidaluz Meneses had her poetry recital a few Wednesdays ago.

My father was in Somoza's Guard, General Meneses.

Vidaluz Menesus was born in Matagalpa, a beautiful town set in the green slopes of a hilly region, now under armed attack by those who are against the revolution. She is a militia member and takes her turn at revolutionary guard duty at the Ministry of Culture. She has a look of peace about herself. Ernesto Cardenal's statement "We have put peace on a war footing" erupts from her lips.

—*For the sake of peace or war?*

She answers without raising her voice, in her normal pleasant tone.

—We've never wanted war. We made war against Somoza to win peace. And now they're forcing us to defend peace. We have to "put peace on a war footing" for the peace of the new Nicaragua because they want to destroy it.

I have to force my imagination to picture her delicate figure toting a rifle over the volcanic soil during militia practice. But alongside Vidaluz's great enthusiasm for the revolution, I'm surprised to learn this fact about her life which she states in a simple way:

—My father was one of Somoza's Guards, General Meneses.

General Edmundo Meneses Cantarero was fatally wounded on the streets of Guatemala, where he was Somoza's ambassador, in September 1978, at the time when the war in Nicaragua against the tyranny was intensifying. Vidaluz was then sheltering Sandinistas in her house and collaborating with the FSLN. General Meneses was shot in the back from a passing car. The Poor People's Guerrilla Army of Guatemala took credit for the attack "in support of the struggle of the people of Nicaragua." At that time Vidaluz felt her heart torn between the two sides of the struggle.

—I was always very close to my father and loved him very much, even though I broke away from his world and opted for the revolution.

—*What kind of love must that have been if you gave up so many things that were vital to your father without rejecting him? How was that possible?*

—Through my Christian faith. The same love that led me to be a revolutionary enabled me to hold onto love even while breaking with my father. Through suffering, but with hope, feeling myself torn apart, and by that very experience being enriched, pulled together, and strengthened.

—*Did your poetry also come into play?*

—Poetry is always part of my life, my faith, my love for my father and my breaking away from him. Now it's part of my revolutionary commitment.

I came to understand this after reading her poem "Last Postcard to my Father," written in 1980 after the revolutionary victory.

> Today should have been your birthday,
> and now you're not here and it's better for you.
> I hold onto your words
> and your parting anxiety
>   about what would happen to me,
> because history didn't let you
> glimpse this moment
>   let alone understand it.
> The verdict is already in.
> I'm telling you that I'm holding close to me
> your generous love,
> your hand on the spoon
>   as you gave your grandson

his breakfast for the last time,
the way you lightened up
the heavy atmosphere of our good-byes.
Each of us on our own side,
like two ancient knights
embracing, before the final—and fatal—duel.

*—You've told me that your poetry is your life —and that poetry is insepara-
ble from the way you live your Christianity and take part in the revolution.*
—As I was finishing high school and lots of things were happening in the
country, you had to become concerned because everything was in an uproar,
the whole crude reality of these Latin American countries of ours. By this time,
I was writing poetry. Ernesto Cardenal, as a priest, came to our school, and
asked for the poems the girls were writing. He chose mine along with others.
Pablo Antonio Cuadra published them for the first time in *La Prensa Litera-
ria.* I was very embarrassed and didn't allow them to print my real name. I
made up a pen name, Vime. They described me as a schoolgirl who was
precociously mature. After that, poetry got me into contact with other groups
of young people who were all raising questions.

When I look back on all those years, from the time I was a young schoolgirl,
I can see that I left my magic religion behind and went on to social commitment
toward a revolutionary change, and that has been connected to my faith in
God, to my Christianity.

> **In this revolution, my poetry is freer and fuller, and my Christianity more
> effective and authentic.**

—My life went on. I got married.
I got my certificate as a secretary and then did pre-university. I didn't know
what I was going to study but I was fascinated by the idea of going to the
university. I didn't go right away because my husband was a student and we
both had to work. I worked all day. I was often uneasy about leaving the kids
for such a long time in order to work, even though we had a lot of family
support. In any case, I always worked, not only because my contribution was
necessary for our family income, but because I felt it was part of my responsibility to society and also for my own personal development. For a long time I
worked in the Central American University. I was always around the university,
sometimes taking courses and getting credit in subjects that interested me. I
was active in student movements and also as a worker in the university.

The whole story is quite long, but the point is that as the result of several things the university went into a crisis. As a worker I signed a statement denouncing a long list of things, and as a student I joined the strike. The rector and his sympathizers or sycophants refused to dialogue and naturally the strike gathered momentum. Not only did we take over the university, but for the first time in the history of Nicaragua people took over churches. In all these events revolutionary Christians were coming together. Everyone played a part. Students, professors, and progressive priests all supported the strike.

> **I was seeking my commitment in society and my marriage went into crisis.**

—After this period I enrolled in the Humanities Department to study library science and graduated four years later. But as I was listening to people from political parties in the university and, almost intuitively, beginning to use political concepts to analyze the situation, including some aspects of Marxism, at the same time I was feeling a lot of anxiety as I realized that my marriage was heading down the well-worn path to becoming comfortably established and bourgeois.

I realized that in our marriage and family life we were following the traditional route of young professional people who buy their house and their car, get themselves set up, and that's where it ends, because they have to defend these possessions. My husband and I talked these things over a lot. But when I analyzed things coldly, I realized that we were coming into conflict, and I think I really put a lot of pressure on my husband. And I realized that sometimes I was increasing my husband's anxiety, when in fact I shouldn't demand that he follow along in the same process I was undergoing.

Perhaps at that point there began a crack that became deeper and deeper as time went on, because we could no longer respond as a couple to what I felt were the real demands of our moment in history. The political and social situation in Nicaragua intensified, and you could no longer maintain ambiguous or anarchistic positions.

In Vidaluz's poems I can see, interwoven with the doubt that impelled her to search untiringly, her dreams, hope, and determination, often wrapped in feelings of creative responsibility toward the future for the sake of her children and her people. "I must hand on to them a world that is wide open and fruitful/ so when they think of me/ they won't say/ my lifetime has been spent in vain." "May no peasant mother ever think/ that my daughter's laughter/ drowned out the sound of her child's sobbing."

—*What role did your Christianity play in your decision to struggle against the Somoza system?*

—For me this whole period was filled with Christian conviction. After the revolutionary victory, I wrote a testimonial in *El Nuevo Diario*. I felt a need and a duty to write it given the way our Sandinista people's revolution was being misrepresented to the public. In my testimonial I showed that in the hardest moments of the struggle the Lord's message had been there to give me encouragement. In the midst of the war, when we were all afraid of the bombing, there was Psalm 91 telling us not to be afraid. When we hid a *compañero* who was on the run, there were psalms that told us with unbelievable clarity that if you hid one who was persecuted, when the oppression was over, a judge who loved justice would come on the scene. And since the victory I've found some things that have happened very moving. I've seen important actions and messages of the Lord fulfilled in our people. An example was the appointment of Amada Pineda to the Tribunal of the Agrarian Reform. She was the courageous peasant woman who announced that she had been tortured and raped repeatedly by Somoza's Guards. At that point I recalled the Magnificat, the verses that say that the Lord has tumbled the mighty from their thrones and raised up the lowly. You see things like that in the revolution, things you experience very directly.

> **I thought to myself, "This will cost either my father's life or my own."**

—My Christian faith supported me in my conflict with my father. This relationship was very painful for me because our feelings were strong and couldn't be ignored. But if you're aware of the real story of Latin America and its struggles you realize that your own case is not unique. Thousands of Latin Americans have had to break off from their families and have had to go through a frightening and painful experience of working things out. The same thing is true here in Nicaragua. My own case was worse because my father wasn't a politician, but a member of Somoza's Guard. My Christian faith helped me. I came to the conclusion that the situation of injustice couldn't continue and that the alternative was quite clear. And when I made my decision for the liberation struggle, I thought to myself, "This will cost either my father's life or my own."

They made my father a brigadier general and retired him after his thirty years of service. This interview is making me probe more deeply into some things. Perhaps along with the corruption of the Somoza regime, it was the fact that my father went back to being a civilian that helped me decide once and for all. A few months after his retirement he was appointed ambassador to Guatemala.

In the first few months of 1978 we got organized in our barrio. I told my neighbors that our Christianity demanded that we be involved in our people's liberation struggle because it was just. We all set up safe houses. I'm sure my father knew I was collaborating with the Sandinista Front. Even though he never asked me directly, our conversations led to the point where I would say that I thought the people's struggle was just.

I knew a student group had written him asking him to resign from his position as ambassador in Guatemala. He never replied. I wrote him a letter talking about the Lord's mercy, about how important it would be for him to take part in a prayer group my mother had joined in Guatemala. I had given up on the idea that he might quit his position, and my final hope was that by becoming more spiritual he would be changed. But history was now moving along at a dizzying pace. My father mistrusted prayer groups because in the Guard the word was that communism was being spread there.

When my involvement in the anti-Somoza struggle was public and there was no turning back, I wrote him a second letter. My mother had told me to explain things to my father because he was getting confused, since I wrote to him with so much love on the spiritual side but my actions were putting him in a difficult situation. So I had to write him a letter that was very painful.

A cream colored envelope of heavy paper, addressed to General Edmundo Meneses Cantarero contains two pages, typewritten on both sides. In the fifth and sixth paragraphs Vidaluz wrote:

Papa, you've been through your life, but I'm in the middle of mine, and my children are just starting out. It was through your sacrifices and generosity that I've had the chance to have a fuller education and to achieve a profession. My education has been basically humanistic, and my own values have had to confront those of the society I live in. At this point I simply cannot become utterly superficial and accept a society where the primary value is economic success, especially when it means running down anyone who gets in my way. Besides that, these structures are so corrupt that to opt for them would mean condemning myself and my children to being accomplices in a whole range of things that are wrong and even criminal.

What I yearn for is a society that is more just and more decent. I don't think I'm being utopian when I believe we can have a better Nicaragua. It is quite clear to me that the change will be (and already is) painful, but my faith rests in the Lord, and I prefer to go through the most bitter period now so my children will really be the "new person" and will be part of a people whose situation has improved.

It was all very painful when they shot my father down. We forgave those who killed him and I offered his blood for the peace of Nicaragua.

—Can I ask you to talk about how your father was killed and what you felt, how you reacted, what your experience during his final hours was?

Vidaluz smiles weakly, half closes her eyes, and speaks with a great deal of concentration.

—On September 16, 1978, as he was going into a barbershop less than two blocks from his house in Guatemala City, my father was shot down. A few days later there appeared a note in the paper in which the Poor People's Guerrilla Army took credit for the action, calling it a gesture of solidarity with the struggle of the Nicaraguan people.

I remember that that day at the morning mass in the parish Father Jacinto Alegre had passed out sheets of paper on which we all committed ourselves to being part of a prayer chain for peace. My part was the fifteen minutes from 12:30 to 12:45 in the afternoon. And it was at exactly 12:30 that an uncle of mine gave me the news from Guatemala. That was a horrible blow to me. The moment had come, and it had hit my father. Months later, I thought about how significant it was that the word had come when it did, and I felt that the Lord had let me know at that moment so that I had to rely on the power of prayer.

The next day I went to Guatemala with my younger sister and one of my children. My father held on for two weeks. During the first week he seemed to be recovering, but if he had lived he would have been an invalid, unable even to sit up, since a bullet had gone into his spine.

I should say that despite the tremendous blow this was for our family, as soon as I arrived, we met in a room, and after saying hello to my father, who had already come out of his operation, we agreed that if Christ, who had been the most perfect human being and had no blame whatsoever, could forgive, we had no reason for not doing the same thing. And from that moment we forgave the killers, whoever they might have been.

It was all very painful, but in a way, I felt relief. I felt that great power of liberation that in some cases can only come from death. I sincerely believe that this is the Christian meaning of death.

> **I buried the memory of my father and took on the commitment to my people forever.**

—When we came back to Nicaragua, all of us, my husband and my children, my married sister and her family, my mother and my other sister went to live at a place in the country. However, the struggle went on, and I felt I shouldn't be disconnected too long, so we went back to our house. A few days later a Sandinista contact came by and asked us to take in a *compañera*. I said I was completely in agreement with the struggle but asked them to wait a few days, since I was feeling emotionally weak. And then, trying to overcome this personal contradiction and to get some time, I added: "Carlos (my husband) should decide since it's his house too, after all." He answered me, "I want to impress on you that sometimes one hour means somebody's life." So they brought us the *compañera*. I remember she was extremely young. She said she was seventeen, but she looked fourteen. Once she sat down with my daughters on the bed to look at their dolls. I saw her from behind, tiny, with a ponytail, and I was so struck that I said to myself, "In Nicaragua it is the children who are carrying out this war—and it is a just war." From that moment, I took on a commitment forever.

Our house continued to be a safe house. At the moment of victory, I felt called to another type of commitment. I felt that in the hour of victory we should be generous.

Since we had lived through such horrible moments under Somoza's Guard and the bombing, it seemed logical for the Sandinista Front to come in ready to wipe them all out. And the Somocistas rushed to take asylum. My family had had a lot of contact with different embassies where we had arranged for Sandinistas to take asylum when they couldn't stay here any longer. So the Colombian ambassador asked us if we could take in some Somocistas, since they couldn't have them alongside the wounded Sandinistas they had harbored earlier. I felt that was really my task at that moment. I said to myself, "I feel no hatred. On the contrary, it's painful for me to see that there have been so many alienated guardsmen and that they have come to commit such a terrible genocide. But I am perhaps among the few people in Nicaragua, who can be one hundred percent behind the revolutionary struggle, and yet emotionally able to take these people in." I felt that was my commitment as a Christian. My husband agreed. And so my whole house filled up with men, women, and children from Somoza's Guard.

After that, the normal work of the revolution got underway, rebuilding the country, and at that time I felt I had to get myself together. My professional background is library science. I chose that when I had a chance, after having all my children. I was mature by that time, and I decided that I had to choose a technical career that would both put me in the world of books, which is what I liked, and would also be a practical kind of training that at some point would enable me to respond to the needs of my people. I put that in a paper I wrote, that I had chosen this line of work to serve my people better. I sent it to the Minister of Education, Tünnerman, and to Ernesto Cardenal, the Minister of Culture. The poet called me and I went into the Ministry of Culture.

There is always some pain deep down, and you have to assume it. It often puts you in conflict because commitment means you have to break with some people. My own marriage had to come to the moment of decision. That was hard because I had hoped to be married forever, as I had been taught. But I'm also fully aware of people's dignity and I thought that, instead of continuing to hurt each other and to make life impossible for each other, it would be more honest for my partner and me to separate. Our children's situation also demanded that. Now that we're separated, we're friends, and that's healthier.

All this meant one more kind of painful questioning, and in it I found a lot of support in my Christian group. Miguel Ernesto Vijil and I were talking about martyrdom and he said to me, "There's one kind of martyrdom—minimal, if you will—but it cuts and wounds you deeply. It's really not so minimal, these are terrible human problems: that you can't share this perspective, this commitment you've taken on, even with your own mother or with the person you have shared your life with, and you have to come to the point of separation." That's another kind of martyrdom that you have to accept.

There is also an answer for this kind of martyrdom in the gospel, strange as it may seem. In a bourgeois society, family values are incredibly inflated, but they only reach out to these small circles, and that's not very Christian, as far as I can see. As a Christian, I can now see that in a socialist society the family is not played down—far from it. These family bonds are wonderful, marvelous, if they're there. But there is another alliance, one that is much broader: the big family, those brothers and sisters Christ talks about. It is the ability to open up and love people you've never seen in your life, people in the hills and in the barrios. This capability for love, which makes us accept as brothers and sisters so many people beyond our flesh and blood family, is Christian. That's what is proposed in the gospel, and Christ lived it.

—*What does Christian faith have of its own that it can contribute to the revolution to enrich it?*

—As I see it, faith provides idealism, not in the sense of going beyond reality, but in the sense of enthusiasm and power for assuming reality with an awareness of an underlying meaning that makes struggle and sacrifice worthwhile. Christianity gives me ideals, strength, hope. For example, with libraries, at this time when attacks are making everything so hard, workers don't come to libraries to read on their own. So we have a mobile library, a bookmobile that now goes to eight factories. Even during this period of aggression against us, the bookmobile keeps going. Through interviews we know that the people are reading these books and discovering another dimension of the world. The bookmobile brings the workers books for their children, and they're happy because they leave their factory with storybooks for their kids, kids that may never have had access to a storybook before. To me that's justice, that's advancing and achieving the things the people want and need. That's what's all-important for me. When the Lord spoke to the masses he made them feel they had dignity as persons.

Some months later I go to her office. Passing through different rooms, the corners filled with work tables piled high with books, I come to Vidaluz. She is surrounded by posters, signs, and slogans. She gives me some typewritten meditations and prayers and a copy of her most recent poem: "I invite you, and I invite myself/ to live in this paradise/ to repose on the star/ where love itself is beyond us/ unnamable, undefinable, being."

10

TEÓDULO BAEZ CABEZAS

Laboratory Analyst for the Nicaraguan Energy Institute

"I was an exploiter. The gospel tells me to be reconciled with my people. That is why I am a revolutionary"

Teódulo Baez was born June 8, 1927, in Managua. He studied chemistry and pharmacy at the Central University in Managua until the university was closed. He then became manager of his father's farm, which later became his own. He and Jenny Cortés Fernández were married in 1949, and have three married children. In 1968 he went to work at the laboratory of the National Geological Service. He now works in the Laboratory for Physical-Chemical Analysis of the Geothermic Project of the INE (Nicaraguan Energy Institute), a ministry-level position in the government.

●

Teódulo Baez begins speaking to me by stating: "I was a Barabbas, a thief, an exploiter, and a scoundrel. I'm telling you, Teófilo, and that's not the half of it. I was beyond calumny. Anything they might have said about me, hell, it was true. Until I began to be a Christian."

I had been told, "He may use vulgar language, but what he has to say is unique." So now here he is before me, short, sharp features with brown wrinkles and thick glasses. ("They call me 'Triangle-Face.' ") Determined. A tornado of words, exclamations, ironies, and expletives. "You'll have to cut me off," he says. "I start talking and I don't let up."

He speaks with conviction, with heat, with passion. The torrent of his speech carries the force of his heart, his imagination, and his lungs. He raises his thick scratchy voice to a shout. And he lets go a string of cusswords and insults that are commonly heard, a striking example of that direct Nicaraguan language that has gone into testimonial literature and fiction, and even into poetry. (I have taken the liberty of cutting down the frequency of these words, but if they were all eliminated, it would not be Teódulo Baez speaking at all. I've recorded them as they came out [here not translated literally but with English expressions that convey a similar feeling.])—TRANS.

He continues his introduction: "Now I'm a Christian, and as a Christian I'm a revolutionary—all the way, dammit! As a Christian I feel I must support this revolutionary process since, as far as I'm concerned, it's the first time we Christians in Nicaragua can really go to work and act like real Christians. Because this is a process of liberation for the poor."

I went to see him a few days ago at the INE laboratory where he works. The place is a long prefabricated building, whose previous occupiers failed, one by one. I asked if I could interview him. "I can't this afternoon, man. I've got militia drill." He had on a militia shirt, rust-colored, made of rough cloth. "Any day I don't have militia drill I can come by your house after work, at five, and I'll be available as long as necessary."

I have him here in the parlor of the parish house in Las Palmas. "This is the church where we used to have our Cursillo ultreyas [follow-up sessions after the cursillo weekend]."

Teódulo looks at me. "Ask anything you want."

He has arrived carrying two Bibles, wearing a small FSLN insignia on his shirt collar.

●

Q—How are you taking part in the revolution?

Baez—I'm a CDS [Sandinista Defense Committee] coordinator, a member of the Sandinista Barrio Committee. I'm trying to help wherever the people need help. I'm in the People's Militia and in all the programs that require help for increasing production. And in all these things, I'm there as a Christian.

I work in the Central Laboratory for Natural Resources. I do physical-chemical quantitative analysis of water in one department of INE, the Nicaraguan Energy Institute, which belongs to the state. I'm in the department of Geothermic Resources. Our job has to do with drilling geothermic wells, seeing where geothermic development might be feasible. I tell my coworkers we have to do this work conscientiously, with all our effort and all our love.

—How do you practice your Christianity now?

—My basic Christian practice is to struggle to live the gospel. To live it, see what I mean, to live it! Lots of people call themselves Christians out of inherited custom or because of religious ceremonies they take part in. I have struggled to get rid of my own routine Christianity. Living the gospel is tough, Teófilo. It's almost impossible but it can be done, it can be done with the help of the Lord. Living a Christianity of complete love, of being brotherly and sisterly. Only someone who works building up something like that can imagine what it is to be a church of brothers and sisters, all children of the same God.

And you know what the secret is? I call it "Operation Tortilla." Someone can tell me, "So-and-so's oldest child was just killed in an accident—such a good kid." "What a goddamn shame!" So I go over to the house and I hold the person and say, "I'm very sorry." But only by being in their place, if I see my own child die, will I really understand. Well, only a person who lives the real story of his or her oppressed brother or sister, dying of hunger, only one who has the experience of becoming poor, only the person who becomes incarnate with the poor like Christ, who became flesh, became human to save human beings (hell, that's what's so spectacular about Christ's faith!)—that's the only way to do it. Operation tortilla: put yourself in their place, dammit, so you can live and feel the same thing. Otherwise, we can't talk about Christianity.

—Tell me about your early Christianity, your childhood. And changes in your Christianity up to the present.

—Don't get the idea I've always been a good Christian. My parents were believers, Catholics. They had me educated in the Colegio Rubén Darío, which was run by religious. I went to Mass and took part in Father Ramírez's Apostolic Action group. I was always involved in church movements. As a kid I made the First Fridays. Then I went to the Pedagogic Institute run by the Christian Brothers. I kept going to Mass, but my Christian life was one of custom and tradition. Maybe that was why I did all kinds of terrible things after I was married. I thought I could do anything and by going to Mass and saying a rosary I was in great shape as a Catholic. I thought I was doing my duty. I was unaware of the gospel and never opened it.

In my marriage, I was a Barrabas, Teófilo, I was a disaster. A complete disaster. I drank booze every day and I was always looking for a way to go out to the farm with some chick I picked up. And I was an exploiter, a bandit, a thief, always squeezing it out of my workers, paying them miserably. That was true until thirteen years ago when I met the Lord in a Cursillo de Cristiandad. I met him and I tell you that the same thing happened to me as happened to St. Paul, because my whole life changed after that. After I made my cursillo, February 13 to February 16, 1969, all that was finished. The Lord gave me will power (I didn't do it myself), and enabled me to establish a Christian home, a "domestic church," where my wife has been everything to me. My children saw the change and they appreciate me for it. Since then I have been a leader at twenty-eight cursillos. I am a sinner but I went to give my testimony.

But I realized that this isn't everything. Being faithful to my wife, forming a domestic church with my children and with my in-laws when my children got married, this was all a bit of heaven, but there must be something more.

From the time I understood love as it is in the gospel, I've seen only one way to go: to end what causes hunger and institutionalizes inequality and privilege.

—When I came out of the cursillo, hell, anyone who came by my house, shoeshine kids, a gardener, anyone, I brought them in and they had a cup of coffee, or had lunch or supper with me. I was so full of Matthew 25.

Once, a few months before the revolutionary victory, I left my office and went to a house where you could buy lunch. A gardener came by and asked for a five-peso meal and the woman laughed at him, "Hey, what do you think this is? Five pesos' worth of food!" "OK, I don't mean to cause trouble," said the gardener and he started to go away. So I called him and said to the woman, "Matilde, give him a meal and something cool to drink." And I ate and chatted with him. On my way back to the office I was meditating, "I was hungry and you gave me to eat." At first I was content: "What I did is just what the Lord wants!" But then I saw him telling me, "Triangle-Face, don't be an asshole. This sort of thing is a band-aid. It's just cursillo stuff if you stay at this level." That was how I realized that Matthew 25, "I was hungry and you gave me to eat," was not just for the kind of band-aids we were used to putting on.

This other saying of Christ, "You are all children of the same Father," also opened my eyes. During the insurrection I lived next to Bosques de Altamira and once I went along with a young woman we had in our house to leave food for her family. In the house next door, there was a shrunken little girl who was dying, starving and dehydrated. So I started thinking. If our God tells us, "You are all children of the same Father," why were my children being fed with seven or eight bottles of milk a day, so much in fact that it gave them diarrhea, while the children of workers and peasants couldn't get even a single bottle of milk, but just water, and got sick and died of dehydration?

When I understood these two gospel passages well ("You are all children of the same Father" and "I was hungry and you gave me to eat") I understood that the gospel and Christianity were not something foreign to the real life and suffering of human beings, and especially were not foreign to what was going on in our own time. I understood that the gospel is a project to undertake, or a proposal, and that we have to make it effective in history. Since that time there has been only one road for me: to end everything that causes hunger and everything that tries to justify and institutionalize inequality and privilege. Now do you see why I told you that this revolutionary process is how we Christians can thoroughly embody Christianity for the first time in Nicaragua?

It's useless to talk about love in the abstract and without works, like the way you hear it in so may homilies from our pastors and our archbishop. They talk about love a lot—"love!"—but always in the abstract. What does love mean in terms of concrete deeds affecting the reality we are living? I became convinced that if the world we are living in, Nicaraguan society, has set up two groups of people, those who have everything and those who have nothing, those who stuff themselves and those who die of hunger, we simply have to go through a struggle between these two groups.

So what they call "class struggle" is something clear and obvious to me. The term might scare some people, but it is an objective phenomenon we are experiencing in the world, in the Americas and in Nicaragua. Class struggle is not a Marxist invention or a thing of the devil. If society is divided into classes (ours has been and still is), *that* is what is diabolical, having two classes so unjustly unequal. Some people want to leave things the way they are and turn their eyes away from injustice and the cruelties it causes. They don't want to struggle. They want things to go on as usual, so they can go on their way. That's twice as diabolical. And they call themselves Christians, some of the people who want things this way. I think the great mission of the church in this world is to end the unjust division of human beings into two classes, rich and poor, because it has to preach, and practice, and spread throughout society Christ's message in the gospel: "You are all children of the same Father," you are all brothers and sisters. If there are two classes that are not brothers and sisters because some have stuffed themselves and others are hungry, we Christians have to take sides. Mary did that and she told us how God does it too, in Luke 1:52–53.

He searches in his big Jerusalem Bible and reads to me:

—"He has pulled down princes from their thrones and exalted the lowly. The hungry he has filled with good things, the rich sent empty away." That was Mary speaking—so let's not be shocked!

Now we Christians have a historic opportunity in Nicaragua; we want to be honest and authentic and to live the gospel seriously. I mean supporting the process of liberation of the poor even though some may scream at us and be scandalized at the mention of "class struggle." Some say, "Class struggle I can accept, but class hatred?" But who is it that has sown class hatred? Hasn't it been us, the bourgeoisie, those of us who have everything, the privileged, who are class-centered? Wasn't I sowing hatred when my children went to a good school in a good bus, and were well fed, while the cook's son was waiting for leftovers, and then went out on the street with his shoeshine kit? Didn't I sow hatred among peasants by robbing them, paying them starvation wages? Didn't I sow hatred, doing what I wanted to pretty girls, destroying their virginity and abusing them? Didn't we sow hatred? And why are we shocked now when the poor claim what belongs to them in justice and what has been denied them for so long?

It makes me laugh, Teófilo, when they talk so much crap. "Ohhh, Triangle-Face, you're a Christian and a cursillo leader, and you've become a Marxist." I don't know shit about Marxism, and less about Leninism. I don't want to understand it. What I use to guide my life is this!

He holds up his Bible.

—My guide for life is the Word of God in the Bible and that's more radical than Marxism-Leninism. The gospel is stronger in demanding that I struggle for justice than Marxism-Leninism. That's why lots of Christians are unaware of the pure gospel.

Are some people talking about the new human being? What a shock for some Christians! What a shock for some hierarchies! Well, let them read St. Paul! St. Paul demanded that two thousand years ago.

And he reads from his Bible:

"You must lay aside your former way of life and the old self which deteriorates through illusion and desire, and acquire a fresh, spiritual way of thinking. You must put on that new man created in God's image, whose justice and holiness are born of truth." Notice what it says, Teófilo: You must "acquire a fresh, spiritual way of thinking" to become a new human being. You have to forget your privileges, you have to give. We have to share what we have, we have to allow the poor to have the same opportunities that my children had and that those of us who were well off have always had. That's not a small order. It's a revolution that demands a radical change in everything.

When I saw the misery of peasant laborers, I knew that I belonged to the group of those who were exploiting them. So I decided to be reconciled to my people.

—Want to know something else? I take up the gospel and I don't just read it halfway. I keep thinking about it over and over.

A few months after the victory, we had a "red-and-black" Sunday; we went to pick cotton over in Cofradías. And since people over there used to come to pick my crops they knew me. I went down to the end so no one would be bothering me and making me waste time. I wanted to pick a lot, to be useful, since before that, on my own farm, I had never picked cotton, not a bit. I only went to enjoy the girls.

Anyway, I saw several peasants there and we were talking and on our lunch break they offered me some of their food. I saw that they had very little, a bit of beans and tortillas, dry, hard tortillas. I shared their food. Then I got to thinking: I've seen the society where these people live their lives, a society of misery and oppression. I thought: "They are all God's children," and right away I remembered "Leave your gift. . . ." I realized that I was unreconciled with these brothers and sisters, and that I had to go be reconciled with the people, with the poor and suffering, because I had belonged to those who had screwed them. I had been part of a dominant class, supporting and aiding their exploitation. And that is where the Lord illuminated me to make a lifetime decision: to go and be reconciled with the people, with my poor neighbor, to make a radical and lifelong option for the poor.

But reconciliation doesn't mean covering up injustices and thievery, it doesn't mean the kind of tranquilizing that we have always wanted to impose on those who were already held down. I recognized that reconciliation with these people meant destroying everything that keeps people unreconciled, everything that makes exploiters and others exploited. The system, the machinery, structures, my farm, what we have, what we own, does not allow us to be brothers and sisters. We are unreconciled. That's the way it is.

I'm going to tell you something else. It's true that Christian love is universal, for everyone. But in the gospel, the beatitudes are aimed at the poor and the woes are aimed at the rich. Loving the poor means helping them to liberate themselves, helping them get organized so they can assert themselves and defend themselves. Loving the rich means screaming about how they abuse the poor so those rich people can become real persons with no more mechanisms of exploitation. I recognized that this is what reconciliation means. It's what all the privileged members of the bourgeoisie who are not reconciled to the people still have to do. It was not just a matter of being reconciled to my brother-in-law or to my neighbor. That is what impelled me to give up my property and end up poor.

In February 1980 the Lord moved me to call my wife and children together. I said to them, "My ideal, the way I think, what the gospel means to me, is that I should hand over what I have." I told them because part of it was theirs too, of course. And my children answered, "*Papa*, is that the way you think, what you yearn for, and what you dream about? Is that your faith in the Lord Jesus and is that what he is asking you to do? Well, that's the best inheritance you could leave us." That's what my children all said. So I handed over my properties, 343 *manzanas* [593 acres] in Sabána-Grande. Four kilometers in from Las Améri-cas, and it was worth a pile of dough, and with no debts to any bank or savings institution. A week before I was offered 100,000 cordobas to let someone plant cotton there. "No, I'm not renting it, I'm going to donate it to the revolution because you have to share. The gospel demands that I make restitution to the poor, and maybe salvation has come to this house as it did to Zacchaeus. If my children had their opportunities, other children should too." I was content.

I stayed at my job and didn't go around trying to get anything else. I could have made efforts to get a good position since I had donated the farm. I'm sinner enough to be an opportunist. But no—I'll stick with my job. I used to work for the headquarters of the IRENA (Nicaraguan Institute for Natural Resources) laboratories. Now I'm working for the INE Geothermic Resources Department, and since coming here I've been making 3,500 cordobas a month [US $350 at the official exchange rate but much less in practice.—TRANS.]. My wife hustles, she gets around, and she helps by doing this and that. Imagine, we don't go to the movies and don't go out to eat. Before I used to use my salary at this job for buying gifts or silly things, since I got 140, 160, or 180 thousand from my property, but I no longer have that. But the Lord Jesus is wonderful. I'm happy, I'm content, I'm not in need of anything, and I have some marvelous children. If you want to reap, you have to sow. Before, when I had everything, they didn't suffer any need. Now if I need something they help me. So I'm happy and content. Besides, I prefer not to have anything so I can talk, so I can bang away or lash away at those who still have things and are unwilling to share, at those in the bourgeoisie who do not want to be Zacchaeuses.

—*So for you there are no problems, contradictions, or breaks between Christian faith and this Sandinista revolution. What about the criticisms and accusations leveled at you by other Christians who don't see things the way you do? And nuns, priests, bishops? They talk about massification, abuses, repres-sion, dictatorship, atheism, persecution against the church. . . .*

—Those are all the fallacies, lies, calumnies, hypocrisies of the people who don't want to face the challenge of living the gospel. Let them live the gospel and they'll see! If our pastors would only say, "The new self. Look what St. Paul says: You have to lay aside your former way of life. Zacchaeus: you have to return what you've taken and make compensation to the poor. Go be reconciled to your suffering people. Give food to the hungry. All of you be children of the same Father." If they did this it would only be preaching the gospel, and they would be in line with the programs of the revolution. Even if they didn't think so. Even if they didn't want to.

He turns the pages in his Bible.

—"Let each of you look to others' interests rather than to your own." That's Philippians 2:4. And what it says here in a hymn which is a kind of declaration of faith: Paul proposes the example of Christ, his path from God to human being, from rich to poor, from being first to being last, from master to servant. That was Jesus' attitude, and his followers, Christians, should have the same attitude. Our desire to be identified with the most humble, to share with them, is what is most proper to the Christian and to living a real gospel life. This idea of looking to others' interests rather than to your own is what the revolution is calling for: that the dispossessed, the outcast, those who have been trampled down for so long should receive the benefits.

> **Here the struggle is not between believers and nonbelievers, not between Marxists and believers. In Nicaragua our struggle is between the well-fed and those who are dying of hunger.**

—The fact is that we're afraid of the gospel. We don't want to live the gospel and we end up accusing the revolution of being against the basis of Christianity, of being atheistic. But that's a lie! The division and struggle here is not between believers and nonbelievers, not between Marxists and believers. Our struggle in Nicaragua is between those who stuff themselves and those who are dying of hunger, between those of us who've had everything and those who've had nothing. That's all there is to it.

They tell me the leaders of the revolution are not believers. So what? I don't know them, I don't have any dealings with them. I would like to meet any of them to congratulate them, not for either believing or not believing, but for being honest, upright, frank, and not being a jerk. Sure, they don't believe in this jerk of a Christ we've presented them with, but they haven't seen the real Christ in our lives. There's been a weak Christ, and an exploiter Christ who is on the side of the rich and against the poor. The rich manipulate religion, fearful for what it would take away from them. There are passages in the Bible, as you know, like the one about the rich young man, and the one on Zacchaeus, which is the one that most made me think. But find me a place in the gospel where Christ says even one little word complimenting the rich. The rich he was friendly with were those who were converted, like Zacchaeus.

It makes me laugh to see the way the *La Prensa* people manipulate the Virgin, the way the reactionaries manipulate the Virgin of Cuapa, the Virgin who sweats, the Virgin who sends us messages against the Nicaraguan revolution. It makes me laugh because I understand these manipulations, since I did the same thing during my Barabbas days. When I planted cotton and I found I had a big flood of money, 250,000 pesos in my pocket, all for me, I set out to do what I damned well pleased. But the first thing I did was to send off to Spain for a statue of the Virgin of Fatima. That was the time, when I was a bandit, that I began to hang my images, of the Virgin of Carmen, of St. Joseph, of the Virgin of Fatima. I held big processions on the farm. Every Saturday, I brought people out at ten in the morning before paying them, and had them say the rosary. If someone didn't pray the rosary, I didn't pay them. I gave them two hours off on Saturday, but they gave it back to me on weekdays. They paid me back—two times five—ten hours! That was stealing and manipulation. "You promised this to the Virgin, and if you don't do it, she may punish you." And the peasants who were so good, so religious and so ignorant, gave me back two hours on the weekdays. What's that? Manipulation, unscrupulousness, theft. That image of the Virgin is still there in the church at Sabana-Grande. Because of this shameful experience from my Barabbas days, I understand all these manipulations of those who are against the interests of workers and peasants— as I was then—those who are now against the revolution.

I can't throw myself into the revolution and leave prayer aside. Union with the Lord is something vital for me.

—*Do you pray? How much time do you devote to prayer now?*

—You may not believe this, but I pray an hour or so every day. At five in the morning I'm out on the porch in silence, seeing the Lord's greatness. I give thanks to the Lord, I praise the Lord, and I ask for light and strength for everyone, including the leaders of the revolution, so we can go forward with this process in favor of those brothers and sisters the Lord loves most, the poorest, those who have always been forgotten and shunted aside in misery. I read the Bible, the Word of God, and I meditate over it often. I find a lot there.

Three or four times a week, or more if I can, I receive the Body of the Lord. For me the Eucharist is vital. I can't throw myself into the revolution, in different work and tasks, and leave aside prayer and communion. "One who eats my body and drinks my blood has life." For us right now in this country, life means energy for getting things moving, for making things clear, for giving an example of commitment and sacrifice. And I know myself, I've been a tough sinner, a Barabbas, and if I spring loose from the Lord . . . "I am the vine and you are the branches; without me you can do nothing." That's not just empty piety, not just routine, and far from pharisaism. I'm a sinner, as I told you, and this union with the Lord is important to me. We Christians should not forget this when we are up to our necks in revolutionary commitments.

—*Are you still involved with the Cursillo Movement?*

—No, because today the Cursillo Movement is a nest of reactionaries. That's where you'll find the powerful and the privileged, that's where you'll find the bourgeoisie, and the aspirants to the bourgeoisie, those who don't have anything but are still bourgeois. They tell me: "Don't call me bourgeois, the bourgeoisie all went to Miami." Not true. I recall something José Coronel Urtecho wrote; "The bourgeoisie as an attitude is a mental or moral disease that sometimes infects other classes."

The last time I was called to help with a cursillo was in 1980. I'm no good to them anymore because all they see in the way I live and in what I tell them is Marxism. They don't see the gospel. Nevertheless, I believe I've filled out and deepened my conversion and my witness to the gospel, incarnating my faith in the Lord Jesus in this people, becoming reconciled to the poor majority that I used to exploit. They don't see the gospel going this far, because they're blinded by their interests and their system which runs against the revolution. Marxism? The gospel! Stupid jerks!

Now I belong to Christians in the Revolution. And my apostolate is with groups of young people, working alongside a priest, organizing a kind of youth cursillo running from Thursday to Sunday.

I was the first one to join a group that went on a retreat in order to form the City of God. I now consider the group to be a sect. I wanted to create a community that would do something for the poor. This was before the revolutionary victory. During the insurrection we were meeting at the house of Doctor Leopoldo Torres, near where I live. Several big names were there, "Chino" Mejía, Humberto Belli. The house stood on a hill and one of Somoza's helicopters was going around dropping bombs on the barrios of Managua. "Son of a bitch!" I said. "They're killing people, children and innocent people. They're killing children of God, our brothers and sisters. Somebody should get rid of the asshole with a bazooka shot!" So Humberto Belli and Chino Mejía said to me, "What's this, Triangle-face? As a Christian can you want something like that? You have to pray, pray that they be converted." "You're all a bunch of goddam sons of bitches!" I said to them. "How am I going to pray for them to be converted if they're killing. What we have to do is ask the Lord for the fall of this asshole because that would be a lesser evil and would end this massacre. Do you see how many people they're killing? How can you be so unconcerned about how many innocent people are being killed and you even want them to go on killing and we can pray to see if they're converted?" We had a fight and I never went back to the City of God. I said the hell with them and didn't go back. From that time on I've been waking up to all I've been telling you about those gospel passages that made me opt for the poor.

I came to see that as a Christian I had to be committed with all my might to the poor, the outcast, the exploited, to those who have never had a chance for anything, for those who got screwed because they never had a chance to learn. "Dammit!" I said, "This revolutionary process is what can give us a chance in history to create a new society and a new kind of person!" A classless society, right? Because what's going on here is not just exchanging one president for another, or one oppressing class for another. No! We want a society where we will live without injustice and without privilege, where we can really be brothers and sisters and all live in communion with God. That's how it's been with me since that time.

One thing I'm convinced of after thinking a lot about the past and present of Nicaragua: You can't live the gospel and be a real Christian, here and now, without being revolutionary and Sandinista.

—*Why "and Sandinista"? Can't you be a revolutionary without being a Sandinista?*

—You can be a revolutionary without being Sandinista in other places. Here and now, in Nicaragua, you can't be a revolutionary without being Sandinista.

Teódulo Baez had many other things to say, all along the same lines, crystal clear and incisive. And he said them bluntly in his rapid and unstoppable style full of characteristic Nicaraguan expressions.

11

FRANCISCO LACAYO

Vice-Minister of Culture

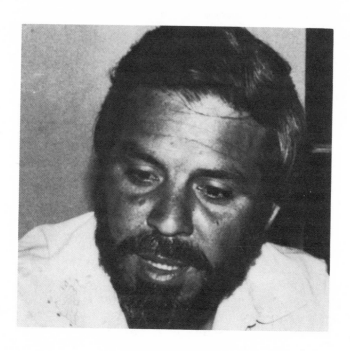

"I'm someone who aspires to be a revolutionary and aspires to be a Christian"

Born in Managua in 1942, Francisco Lacayo joined the Christian Brothers in Liguria (Italy) in 1960. He studied at the Pontifical University of Salamanca (Spain) in 1962, and from 1963 to 1967 in Panama. Upon returning to Nicaragua in 1968 he was appointed principal of Colegio La Salle in León. He started the Christian Youth Movement, many of whose members joined the anti-Somoza struggle. In 1969 the Guardia killed his nephew Mauricio Hernández. After this he left the congregation and went to France. After studying sociology and psychology in Montpellier, he came back to Managua in 1973. At the National University he taught psychology. There he became more involved in the anti-Somoza struggle and by 1977 he was collaborating with the FSLN. Prior to the insurrection, Bishop Pablo Vega asked him to organize the Justice and Peace Commission of the Bishops Conference. For family reasons he went to Mexico with his wife and two children in 1978, and they lived there during the war of liberation. After the revolutionary victory, he held a position in the Nicaraguan Embassy in Mexico. He then worked in the Foreign Ministry in Managua. He was part of the coordinating team of the literacy campaign and in 1980 became the Vice-Minister of Adult Education. Since October 1982 he has been the Vice-Minister of Culture.

●

The first time Francisco Lacayo arranged a day and a time for an interview with me, he was Vice-Minister of Adult Education. The interview was repeatedly postponed because of his heavy workload. Finally one morning I came into his office at the time we had agreed on, but an unexpected rush of urgent situations forced him to ask for one more postponement. Meanwhile he was appointed Vice-Minister of Culture, and I've had to wait until he has been able to catch up in his new assignment.

I'm now in his office in the downstairs part of this unusual site for the Ministry of Culture, Somoza's old mansion, set in the middle of a large piece of property called El Retiro. The Vice-Minister's office is at the foot of the stairway that leads up to the nest occupied by the Minister of Culture, the poet Ernesto Cardenal.

I've taken advantage of the few moments while we're being served coffee and Francisco is talking on the phone to look around the room but I can't take in so many photos (faces of ordinary people, groups involved in the literacy campaign and adult education), paintings, plants, ceramics, various art objects, wall decorations, and so forth. The Vice-Minister has asked that no more calls be let through, and we're now getting into the interview. The utter intensity Francisco pours into his answers forces me to make an extra effort to concentrate. I ask him to speak about his witness as a Christian in the revolution.

●

Lacayo—Giving witness to the values one believes in, those one lives for and will probably die for, one does that every day as something normal. But to have to suddenly talk about that witness so that it will be written down somewhere, to entrust it to you so it will be set down permanently in a book, that's something that breaks my usual patterns. It's the kind of thing one hasn't planned and never thought of doing. But just like many things in life that one never planned to do or thought of doing, one has to take it on and do it.

His face is dark and he has a deep scar on his cheek. His eyes are ebony, his hair and beard dark with wisps of white, and his voice forceful and sharp. All this underscores the deep seriousness of his words.

—If I try to locate where I am in the revolutionary process and in Christian faith, I have to say I'm someone who aspires to be a revolutionary and aspires to be a Christian. I think that it's at the end of a person's days when history and the community can finally say who that person was. That's what makes it interesting—it is a process in which until the very last moment the doors are always open for defining oneself further.

Aspiring to be a revolutionary and aspiring to be a Christian means living out these two dimensions as an ongoing struggle and an ongoing process, as something that is never finished and something that disturbs and shakes up that which is deepest in the human person and the relations one has with those around, from one's children to one's colleagues to the people as a whole.

Looking at things from the viewpoint of history, and also as a revolutionary, I think that in this Sandinista people's revolution there is a great and beautiful contrast, one that is perhaps unique at this time, between how small we are as a people, in terms of economic resources, population, and land area, and how great we are, in terms of creativity, originality, struggle, firmness, clarity, hope, and our conviction about the history we are building up, a universal historic consciousness. It's as though with the victory of the Sandinista people's revolution, the whole world, all humankind, suddenly made its way into the heart of the Nicaraguans. We are taking into ourselves all the struggles, sufferings, hopes, and triumphs of the oppressed of yesterday, of today, and of tomorrow, and that has made our hearts swell enormously. We have grown in order to measure up to what history demands, without ceasing to be small.

We are living that same experience, many of us, in another dimension, in our experience of faith. And along with faith, and as part of it, is that dimension of Christian life that I especially like to refer to because I think it is something essential to Christianity: hope. There's a lot of talk about commitment and love, and there's a lot of talk about faith, but the catechism used to say there were three great virtues, faith, hope, and charity. Perhaps our present experience in history is leading us to understanding of this dimension of hope greater than we've ever had before, this assurance that the revolution is greater and more powerful than we are, and that this faith we experience in the Christian community is greater and stronger than we are.

I recall a line that has often served as a reference point in my life at those moments when the temptation in the face of history, the temptation for Christians, is to be discouraged, to give up our mission in history out of despair and discouragement, timidity, cowardice, and withdrawal. The one who first made me listen to this phrase as something relevant was a great man, Roger Shutz, prior of Taizé. It comes from St. John: "Although my heart condemns me, God is greater than my heart." Along with the certainty of our weakness, we also have the certainty that a strength greater than our own is leading us.

The contrast is striking. While other interviewees have recounted their life and their experience in the revolutionary process with dates and anecdotes, Francisco Lacayo rarely says "I." He begins with a timid "one" and then moves to "we." The thinking he expresses is essentially collective, but deeply personal at the same time. He has melted into the people and into the collective force that is leading the revolution, but he offers personal angles of experience and a reflective assessment that few others are capable of providing. He puts himself at some distance, but does not lose that passion with which he has taken on both the revolutionary cause of a people whose experience and values are quite remarkable and a Christianity that is evangelically postconciliar.

I used to say to Shutz that there are two great bearers of the Christian message who are often disregarded: the poor, the oppressed, those who speak another language, those who have no rank; and those who were called "just pagans" in early Christianity. From my viewpoint as a Christian, the Spirit holds back many things from those of us who try to follow Christ and puts them in the mouth of the poor, in the encounter with the poor and in the encounter with people of good will, that is, those who struggle for justice and for peace in this life, in our own history.

Our audacity is tremendous, the audacity of the poor who know they are right and who, whether they are believers or unbelievers, know that truth will ultimately be victorious.

—How do you see the relationship between the faith of Christians participating in the revolution and the revolution itself? Do the values of this faith and this revolution influence each other?

—I think many of us have to confess that in this revolution we've received more than we could have hoped for in our life. Many of us, myself in particular, have had the privilege of making our modest contribution to tasks that are very important and of experiencing a fruitful relationship between Christian faith and revolution. The Sandinista people's revolution is something quite original and it has values that are peculiarly its own. There's no point in discussing whether these values come directly from the presence of Christians in the revolution or not. It's enough that they're there. Our revolution has shown the world a real commitment to the oppressed, to the poor. The price has been paid in blood, in daily struggle, in wholehearted dedication, in honesty. A relentless commitment led the Sandinista National Liberation Front to spend twenty years struggling without making any deals that would have betrayed its principles and its commitment to the people, without seeking an easy share in political power that it could have gotten.

Our programs have entailed a whole series of decisions that any person of good will, any person who believes in justice and seeks it honestly, would have to agree with. In these decisions our point of reference has been, and continues to be, a clear philosophy of the value of the human person. I think anyone would have to be impressed by our revolutionary attitude toward our enemies. What I mean is, in general, a deep respect for the human person in the midst of a fierce struggle against the evil in structures, against the evil in dictatorship, against imperialism—not out of fanaticism, but because all that has in fact caused a lot of bloodshed, suffering, deaths, misery, ignorance. And that's why we have to struggle.

I've gone through several different experiences. One of them was in the field of diplomacy, right after victory. An interesting experience, one that I lived as an aspirant Christian and revolutionary. The problem was how to live with authenticity in that world of diplomacy. I did it for a short time, first in Mexico and then here in the Foreign Ministry. My experience was that you can in fact live with authenticity in that world of diplomacy, which has traditionally been a world of lies. It was my experience that, with all our smallness, our greatest power came from the truth—without falling into naiveté, naturally.

> **Both in the revolution and in Christian faith, it is deeds that matter, and by our deeds we will be judged.**

—Often in our struggle we've shared the deepest human experiences with *compañeros* and *compañeras*, without asking whether or not they believed in Christ or in God. These shared, deep experiences have enabled us to avoid many theoretical discussions. Ultimately, in both the revolution and in Christian faith it is deeds that matter; our deeds judge us.

For example, in the National Literacy Crusade, in which I aided in the coordination and direction that had been entrusted to Father Fernando Cardenal (a brother whom both Christians and revolutionaries hold in high esteem here in Nicaragua) we saw no contradiction between our faith and the revolutionary process. On the contrary the two experiences nourished one another. The idea that the inspiration for understanding where the road is going is in the power and purity of the interests of the masses of the people was one of the great forces propelling the literacy crusade, getting a people on the road in a process of liberation. Anything theology books might have to say about rediscovering this line of thought about a people on the march, the revolution as a people on the march—Nicaragua lived it all deeply during the National Literacy Crusade. The facts are quite clear: a half million people learned to read and write through the work of the young people who lived with them out in the hills. We paid a very high price: fifty-nine heroes and martyrs fell in this struggle.

> **Meeting nonbelieving *compañeros* who gave up their life for the people nourished our faith.**

—My next experience took place in the Adult Education Program. That's also a program with a great deal of Christian and revolutionary boldness: it is breaking a whole series of patterns, democratizing the teaching function so that the people themselves can take part; the slogans that "one who knows something should teach one who knows less" and "the people teach the people" stopped being demagogic as they had been in other places and became something real. And so we've come to the point where we have 24,000 volunteer "popular teachers," peasants, housewives, children (most of them, about 80 percent, are from the popular classes), who are day by day teaching their brothers and sisters.

Such an experience would be impossible in a country as poor as ours unless the people have extraordinary qualities. I think we're the only country that has more popular teachers than school teachers. There are about 24,000 popular teachers and some 18,000 school teachers. The fact that this is possible three years into the revolution, that the country is covered with education collectives (which are not schools—in fact we're not interested in classifying them and finding a name for them), that we are in a state of education or a process of education—that's as great as the event of Moses liberating the people of Israel from Egypt. This event that we read in the Bible presented as an extraordinary event, a man and a people liberating themselves from aggression, with horrible things happening all around, setting off toward the promised land—we are living that event just as much or perhaps more, who knows? It is so easy to understand many things in the gospel on the basis of this revolutionary experience! I think that a bishop, a priest, or a religious who experienced the National Literacy Campaign or the National Adult Education Program, this mobilization of the people toward their liberation, culture becoming a mass movement, would find it easy to understand many things that aren't understood well in seminaries and theology departments.

Many of us here who profess to be believers and Christians were taught a fearful faith, a faith that was not aware enough of the power of the Spirit of Christ. So we protected that faith, we were on the defensive toward those who didn't believe, and everywhere we looked we saw something diabolical. We forgot that above the evil, and much stronger than the evil, stood the action of the Spirit of Christ. In the revolution, we've had to live together with all kinds of coworkers, and they all have something that creates community: their belief in certain human values. And so all that fear disappeared. Not only did meeting nonbelieving *compañeros*, people who were offering their life for the people, not turn out to be something negative for our faith, but in fact it was deeply nourishing for that faith. To see both the believer and nonbeliever fall in the same trench, sacrifice their life with rifle in hand, or teach people to read and write, or work in health campaigns, and do these things for the same concrete human persons, for our children, for our women, for our peasants, for the most beautiful part of our people, the oppressed—that is enriching for anyone.

It's a continuing challenge and it purifies Christians of any "imperialistic" temptation. It makes us realize that ultimately it is not we who give the faith and that only in the end will we come to understand what the specific mission that Christ has entrusted to us really is. It purifies Christians of all pride and elitism. All of us, people with faults, we are all enriching one another, equal in the struggle, all just as likely to get weary and betray our people. But we also have the same chance to become great by sacrificing ourselves for our people and for all the peoples of the world. It is a very marvelous thing to discover this process of mutual enrichment between believers and nonbelievers, each respecting the other.

> **I think our abnegation and willingness to serve are a witness and an experience that should help the church community rediscover Christian poverty.**

—That brings to mind another value that is important as we live our revolution: the openness with which we try to throw ourselves into this revolutionary process so that it will transform us and turn us into new people. It purifies us, it makes us part of the common people, in the most beautiful and most positive sense of that expression. This continual openness, day by day, year by year, means being present and committing ourselves in whatever way the liberation struggle of the oppressed demands. So you give up making plans that might bring some stability (but also make the world revolve around you). You no longer know what house you're going to live in and what house you'll die in. You give up plans for a career, further study, particular kinds of jobs, you give up lots of things.

This even applies to the international aspect of revolution. We're going beyond the idea of the nation. We know that some day borders will be erased and that our homeland—maybe also our grave—will be any bit of land where people are struggling for justice and for peace. That seems to be so much a part of the value of Christian poverty. Our understanding of Christian poverty used to be so small-minded, something to soothe your conscience. In fact Christian poverty means the readiness to sacrifice everything, even what you have struggled for, like Abraham sacrificing Isaac.

Contrary to the hullabaloo raised by some churchmen, our revolution is helping the people assume their religious traditions.

—My most recent responsibility has been in the area of culture, an area that our revolution cherishes and promotes. Again I have had many experiences as I've gotten into the tasks of the revolution's cultural programs alongside people as great, in every way, as Ernesto Cardenal and our other great creative people. It is a luxury for our revolution to have had a Ministry of Culture. It is a deep affirmation of the revolution. It shows the attention we want to give to our people's roots and to their creativity and artistic expression.

One of the greatest values of the Nicaraguan people is undoubtedly creativity. The people are very creative. If we think of it from a Christian viewpoint, creativity is also one of the things that defines what is Christian. The new person we all want to build up, all people of good will, must be profoundly creative. Creativity is struggle, it is boldness, it is taking the risk of making mistakes, not being afraid to make mistakes. It is the unity of our past with our present and our future. Our starting point for being creative is what we have inherited, what we have done. Starting with what we are, we are building our future.

This is related closely to the question of tradition and of the evolution of the church in history, the question of faith as gift, process, and history. In this cultural and ideological realm, the Sandinista people's revolution, far from slighting or rejecting our past, our traditions, including religious traditions, actually safeguards them. Not only does it respect them, but it is providing the means for purifying them and rescuing what is liberating in them.

Contrary to all the hullabaloo some churchmen make, when they come to a stereotyped and small-minded conclusion that "We're on our way toward atheism" and who knows what else—as though atheism could be planned—despite all this noise from certain churchmen, our revolution and our leaders are providing our people with a chance to assume their own religious traditions. We know that within these traditions there are elements that will fall by the wayside, since they will gradually be purified and transformed. A whole series of degenerations was mixed up with religious traditions, resulting from exploitation—drunkenness, for example. Getting drunk was a sort of religious rite according to the customs of the people, who found there an escape valve for their sufferings and misery. Our revolution now safeguards religious traditions and at the same time is beginning to eliminate aberrations like drunkenness.

The revolution even respects and safeguards some religious traditions that many of us who are Christian believe aren't the most authentic expression of our faith. But here the revolution gives us a good example: respect for tradition, provided we help our people take on that tradition with a growing awareness and maturity in a continual purification process. That's why our processions still go on, our people's celebrations, all these traditions that have different functions, not just religious ones. They are a kind of social salary for our people, entertainment. They allow the people to be happy and celebrate.

—*There are sectors of the church, including much of the Nicaraguan Catholic hierarchy, that don't see the participation of Christians in the revolution as such a positive thing.*

—That's true. There is such a thing as moral and ideological power. Churchmen have had it here, and still do. But the revolution comes along and it has not only political authority but moral authority as well. The revolution, revolutionary values, and the Sandinista Front issue a call to our people, and the people set out on the march. At that point some churchmen feel that the revolution is competing with their moral authority, and instead of being happy with this growth and with the emancipation of the people, they're afraid of it and view it as a danger. But it isn't a threat to the faith—it's a threat to their status. What's in crisis in these Latin American societies as they go into revolution is the status of churchmen.

We know this is very hard for them, since it means the death of this "class" of men in the church. But they will be saved as persons and as believers only if they die to their status in order to be reborn with the people. That is a challenge. For them it is a moment of grace, as the theologians would say.

> **Our people practice a living ecumenism around the interests of the poor.**

—I'm impressed by the ecumenical process taking place in Nicaraguan Christians in the midst of the revolution. Our people never really understood why the churches in Europe had split up because they split over what people experienced over there, in those historic social and political struggles. Here the oppressed assimilate those divisions without having taken part in them. They were imposed on us. And now, in the revolutionary process, with no great theological discussions or seminars, suddenly, in a way that is spontaneous and vital, we Christians from the different separated churches, are coming together around the interests of the poor. These interests of the poor, which bring us together, are creating among us an ecumenical process that is simple and yet as vital as any that has taken place anywhere. Persecution by those who are

against the interests of the poor pulls us together, as does the purifying struggle
to surrender our life for our people.

*—I stop the tape recorder, without knowing whether we've finished the
interview.* "Enough for now. I'll transcribe it and send it on to you, and then
we'll see."

—I'd like to ask you a favor, Teófilo. *Francisco looks at me. I nod and wait.*

—Some day when you have time, I'd like you to come bless this office, and
also my house, which hasn't been blessed.

*This isn't what I expected. I'm surprised and I don't know if I look a little
perplexed or amazed. He must notice that because despite the fact that I agree
he explains his request with some insistence.*

—I believe in blessings. I believe in them out of faith. To me a blessing is one
of the deepest things in Christianity when it is done right, with people getting
together, praying together, and with faith and openness, invoking God's presence, his benevolence, his love.

*Later I see Francisco, but hurriedly. He's on his way to Europe, as part of his
job.*

12

ZELA DÍAZ DE PORRAS

President of the Second Regional Appeals Court

**"As Christians, my husband and I opted for the revolution in
order to create just structures in Nicaragua"**

*Zela Díaz was born in Chinandega on September 22, 1932. She is a lawyer
and a notary. In 1954 she married Alonso Porras, a surgeon. They have seven
children. From 1965 to 1977 Díaz was a legal advisor for small farmers
cooperatives and for the hospital and school for Special Education in Chinandega. She was involved in the foundation and the work of the Apostolic
Institute for the Family and became a member of the pastoral council of the*

117

*diocese of León in 1972. Since 1981 she has actively promoted Christians in the
Revolution. In 1982 she helped form a group for reflection and apostolate in
Chinandega. From 1973 onwards she and her whole family collaborated with
the Sandinista Front. She is a founding member of AMPRONAC (1977) and
AMNLAE (1979). In 1981 she was appointed Magistrate of the Appeals Court
in León and in 1983 President of the Second Regional Appeals Court.*

●

*I take the bus from Managua to León, to interview Zela Díaz, a woman
whom I remembered from the time she gave a report on the problems of her
area at a meeting of church people. I've been told she is now a court magistrate
in León, lives in Chinandega, and is a very active Christian.*

*The bus leaves Managua, going up a hill passing alongside the dry shore of a
lake. The landscape is a striking chain of volcanos. At first it is the perfect giant
cone of Momotombo that dominates, enwrapped in a blue-grey robe, and
breathing out thin curls of smoke through its lips, open and burnt.*

*As we approach León, Momotombo cedes the stage to a row of old volca-
noes, deformed, burned out, dormant, now covered with thick green growth.
And off there behind the city is San Cristóbal with its cone cut off. The huge
mouth, close to the heart of fire inside, throws up dense white steam.*

*In León, once the capital, now foreboding and solemn, you can see the signs
of war. The cathedral and the churches are beautiful masses of stone, gilded,
grey, black. Some churches in León take me back to Castille; others take me
back to the time of the Indians during the evangelization under the conquest.*

*The gardens, the large church, and the market make up the plaza of San
Juan, where, under sun and shade, the crowds lay down their bundles and
burdens at the base of the high wall of the church, or move about through the
market passageways. Stalls and makeshift awnings, big baskets with fruits,
roots, grasses, cheeses, meats, clothing, shoes, kitchenware. The sun filters
through cloth and canvas, there is a pervasive smell of rotting foods, and the
floor is dirty.*

*Right next to this plaza stands the Court or Palace of Justice, where Zela
works during the morning. In a bare room, sitting at a small table she reads or
studies, using a fan to offset the heat. She is short, dark-skinned. Her hair is
black and there are lines around her eyes, which look at me through large
glasses. I listen to what she has to say. Her speech is fluid, cultured, precise, and
quick.*

**I feel fulfilled in my Christian faith, working within this process, in order
to build up the kingdom of God.**

Q—You are a Christian and profess it openly. What is your Christian life like now, your faith and your active struggle on behalf of the gospel?

Díaz—That's right, I'm an active Christian—Roman, Catholic, and apostolic. And it is within this revolutionary process that I am living my faith in its fullness, without the contradictions I had before. I feel satisfied as a Christian, fulfilled in my faith, working within this process, building up the kingdom of God, which is a kingdom of justice and love, and to which we Christians are called. Previously, I felt very bad. As a Christian I felt disoriented, and I shared in the kingdom of injustice and violence. But now the revolution provides us with a great chance within history to show that we are really Christians.

—How do you give explicit profession to your faith as a Christian in this revolution?

—The rejection we felt from the hierarchy and from those sectors of the church that oppose and resist the revolution at first made us withdraw from even going to the liturgy, from taking part in the liturgy in the parish. It was unpleasant to go there and hear a priest denounce as evil and perverse what we thought was good and worth doing. Then we began to feel the need to find other people who felt and thought as we did, and to support others who were moving away because they found no consolation in their faith, due to this rejection from certain members of the hierarchy and groups close to them. That's how it happened that a large number of us, Christians from different parts of Nicaragua who are working in this revolutionary process, have come together, motivated by our Christian faith. We call ourselves Christians in the Revolution. I'm committed to this group, to this movement of Christians.

—Does that name mean you substitute the revolution for the church, that you split from the church or from the bishops?

—No, not at all! We are not splitting off from the church. We are church. We are not breaking off from the hierarchy, from the bishops. That should be quite clear. We call ourselves "Christians" in the full meaning of the term. "Christians" means Christian community, community of faith, it means church. We are not a parallel church or alternative church, as some go around saying in order to discredit us and to avoid dealing with the contradiction that is taking place. We are members and part of the only church there is, a church that is, taken altogether, the Mystical Body of Christ.

The fact that we call ourselves "Christians in the Revolution" is just a way of putting a public name on a presence and a commitment we need to make explicit, as I said, so people will know that, without ceasing to be members of the church—indeed because of it, because we are Christians, followers of Christ—we are within the revolutionary process, along with our people, propelled by our faith. In order to better carry out the gospel option for the poor, to build up the kingdom of God, which is of the poor and primarily for them.

We are simply Christians united in the church, and we accept the authority of our pastors. I mean authority in the strict and Christian sense of the word "authority," since we know that our pastors, as human beings, when they deal

with human matters that aren't dogmas of faith, can make mistakes and can
have their opinions on matters that are open to discussion, such as social and
political systems. We also know that the authority of the church cannot be a
matter of blind imposition, but that reason must come into play in those areas
that should be settled by reason. We think our pastors do not lose authority if
we disagree with their opinion on things that are matters of opinion and open to
discussion. We aren't disparaging the pastoral authority and the role of our
bishops when we disagree with some of their stances when it doesn't affect
aspects of the faith that are dogma or beyond discussion.

We experience a need to make our faith explicit and that's why we meet and
have given ourselves a name. We have seminars, we discuss things, we form
communities and join together in reflection groups with other Christians who
have the same concerns. When you are immersed in reality, and especially in a
reality that is as all-absorbing as the revolution, if your faith doesn't get
feedback in community with other Christians, you'll gradually lose the dimension of transcendence, of meaning, of why you're here.

*We've gone to Chinandega. At one in the afternoon we arrived in the jeep of
one of Zela's coworkers. I'm in her house. A big old family house, rather
colonial, with its inside patio, green and square, full of plants. Also in the
house are Zela's husband, Doctor Alonso Porras, some of their children, the
grandmother in the rocking chair, the dog. The hot air bears the sounds of
family life. Outside, right at the doorway, the market fills the street: stalls
loaded with vegetables and fruits, vendors, and the people with their noise,
voices, and smells. "They bombed the market during the war, and at the time of
the revolutionary victory, the vendors came and took over these streets. They
completely surrounded our house, and blocked us off. Since the heat makes
you leave everything open, the noises and smells fill the house. You've seen how
you almost have to jump over the stalls to get in the house. Our first reaction
was to resist, to refuse. We can't have this, we said. This is our house. But they
told us: That was before. Now it's not like that. Your house is your house, but
the street belongs to the people, and you can't stop us from making a living
here. They were right. We accepted it and now we appreciate it. We're the same
people."*

—*What kind of Christian education did you have? How did you live your
Christianity before taking part in the anti-Somoza struggle?*

—My theoretical religious education was solid. At that time, no one demanded anything more in Christian practice than being a pure young lady, not
having bad thoughts or bad desires, going out to teach a bit of catechism, and
giving alms to the poor.

However, I've always had a special concern for justice and for the poor. My
father taught me that. From the time I was a tiny child he made me see that all
the people working for you are working for your happiness, and you have to
regard them as human beings and be concerned for them. Once when I was
very small he made me go tell a servant I was sorry. I had answered her back

with an insult. The servant left the house and my father made me go over to her house to say I was sorry and ask her forgiveness. That's why thinking of the poor, keeping them in mind, and somehow being concerned for them is something that took root in me from the time I was very small.

When I graduated from the university I was already married. Through my husband's professional life as a doctor, I began to experience the misery and the injustice suffered by the people. Perhaps I should mention that my doctoral thesis, for a doctorate in law, was on the social doctrine of the Catholic Church. I always had social concerns, and I had to find answers in the faith. I learned that the church had a social doctrine. They didn't teach it in school at the time. So I threw myself into looking for information on it.

Later, I went to Spain for a year of postgraduate study. Existentialism was the rage, and all the students went around with books by Camus and Sartre tucked under their arms. I heard about Teilhard de Chardin there, read him, and liked what he said. The Vatican Council was going on. It was shaking up the church. Then John XXIII died.

In Spain, I lived in a convent of Assumption Sisters. The provincial was a woman who was completely in tune with Vatican II. Being with her alerted me to the renewal of the church, to *aggiornamento*. I began to feel satisfied. I was finding the answer to my concerns. But when I came back to Nicaragua, no one was interested. Coming back to my own church, I found it asleep and empty. There were still priests who celebrated Mass in Latin with their back to the people.

I later came in contact with a Dominican priest who was working in El Salvador. He had ideas about society that were advanced. We had study groups, we analyzed the gospel, and much deeper and more disturbing questions emerged. The gospel gave us answers and we translated them into work projects we carried out with peasant groups. We tried to organize grassroots Christian communities. You should have seen how abandoned the peasantry in Nicaragua was at that time. Their living conditions were subhuman.

We began to help them stand up, to develop awareness and a sense of their dignity as children of God. But when we tried to organize them in community and when they began to awaken and respond themselves, we ran into very serious limits and obstacles. We were going at it with a mindset that went no further than developmentalism, but we ran into the hard fact that we really couldn't develop anything. The peasant could really feel like a child of God, a brother or sister with everyone else, and created with all the dignity of one who is an heir of heaven, and yet that person was dressed in rags, or their child would die because they didn't have any medicine and were undernourished. That began to have an impact on our consciences. Peasants themselves collided with that harsh reality and suffered repression because they claimed their rights. So then they said to us, "OK, now what? I now know all about my dignity and I know they're trampling me down. So now what? When is Moses coming to liberate us?" This sort of thing both challenged and disturbed me.

> **When we laypeople proposed a more conciliar way of organizing pastoral activity, the bishops became afraid and everything came to a halt.**

—During the seventies the idea of *pastoral de conjunto* began to gain ground in Nicaragua. [In Latin America *pastoral de conjunto* means planned, collaborative, systematic pastoral work at the diocesan or even national level, involving priests, religious, and laypeople.—TRANS.] When laypeople were told of their role in pastoral activity, when their importance and their rights in the church were mentioned, they took it all seriously.

The meetings began and the clergy and laity began to question the way the church was organized: how authority functioned and how priests were practicing a form of religion that didn't go beyond sacramentalizing. That didn't please many priests whose ministry was quite mechanical and tied to making money. No doubt they put pressure on bishops, and the bishops felt confused, pressured on one side and challenged on another. They were caught in the middle. We had a big meeting in Managua and you could feel a church that was bubbling. A transformation was taking place in Nicaragua. That was in 1972, Medellín had happened in 1968 [a meeting of the Latin American Bishops Conference], and you began to hear talk of liberation theology. It was a rebirth. A new Christian awareness was emerging, and it began to run up against the old ideas. The hierarchy didn't like all this. Then the earthquake came, and for them it was like being delivered from a nightmare. The bishops forgot all about this systematic pastoral activity they had been seeking. The effort at national pastoral work ended, and from then on, it was at a diocesan level. Things were prepared ahead of time and directed, and there was no longer that creative freedom. It became a sacramentalizing kind of pastoral activity, nothing more.

Later the situation changed completely. The liberating fermentation was stifled. Even though the bishops adopted positions of more or less open opposition to the Somoza dictatorship, whenever it was a question of looking at the gospel in a deep way, or examining the way the church was organized from within, they didn't move forward.

> **We couldn't speak of love in Nicaragua while there was no justice.**

—At that time we believed that the young people who went away to the mountains were communists and had lost their faith. That's how we saw them because that's the vision we had been given in our formation. It was the way people thought in that society and that church and it weighed heavily on all of us. We used to say to the bishops, "There has to be an answer for the young people and for the peasants." But our hierarchy wasn't capable of seeing that. They couldn't or didn't want to see it.

Later, when we were in closer contact with the young people, we felt that what they were doing amounted to a practical response to this anguish and thirst for justice that had been awakened in us and in which we put the whole meaning of our faith. What I mean is that through our own study and through our life and experience with the grassroots, with the poor, we realized that everything remained a dead letter as long as there was no justice, which had to be the foundation for everything. We couldn't speak about love or anything, as long as there was no infrastructure of justice. And when we saw the determination, the generosity, and the self-sacrifice of these young people, we felt that they were a response to this search and this yearning.

From that time on, we opted for the Sandinista Front. Well, when I say "We opted for the Sandinista Front," you're going to tell me that we were substituting the Sandinista Front for Christian faith. But we didn't substitute it. It was out of the motivation of our Christian faith that we made that option, as a way to achieve the transformation of society. Out of our faith we opted for the Sandinista Front's position of struggle, in order to bring about that change toward justice that our faith and the gospel of Christ were demanding for Nicaragua.

Later we realized that the peasants who had said they wanted a Moses reacted just as we did when these young people arrived and told them about the struggle they were undertaking. These peasant folks whose awareness in the faith we had aroused were the first to sign up when the Sandinista Front came. They saw the Front as a response to their yearning for justice. They saw it out of their Christian faith, from their situation of dignity as children of God who were being exploited, cast aside, repressed, and whose rights were being trampled.

We continued with our life of faith, taking part in the sacraments and committing ourselves to the struggle more and more each day. I can tell you that this has been our practice and our idea practically since 1974, and we've tried to bring others around to the same thing.

> **My son checked with us and we advised him to make a choice between being a doctor in a capitalist society or going away to die unknown in the hills.**

—You may be interested to know that our oldest son, Alonso, fought in Chinandega. And I'd like to emphasize that we weren't in the Sandinista Front on account of our son, but on our own. We made our moves at the same time. He did it first in Managua, and then in León at the university, and we did it here in Chinandega. So he didn't influence our decision, and in fact, when he was going to make his decision, he came to talk with us. I think it is significant that a son would come with all his doubts to talk with his parents about a personal decision that for him was like a sacred vocation with the people. We talked it over with him, but didn't tell him to do one thing or another. The important thing was that he feel satisfied, and have a calm conscience. We brought up his future as a doctor since that's what he was studying. He had to choose between being a good specialist, with all the privileges it would bring in a capitalist society and going to the hills, where he would be obscure and unknown. But what he had to figure out is where he would feel fulfilled. At the time he didn't give any answer, since what we said was simply for him to think about. He decided to join the Front.

I want to tell you something important for us, what has been perhaps my greatest suffering as a mother. It was the last day of the September uprising, the day of retreat. The *muchachos* had come at night and told us, "We're going to try to take the command post. Get ready to take care of the wounded. We don't have ammunition so either we do this or they'll get us anyway." In the early morning we heard shots, not at the time they'd agreed on, but much later. And then there was heavy bombing all day. There was a request that anyone who had heavy weapons should go to the command post, but no one went. We thought, "They're trapped." The next day they said the marshes along the river were full of bodies. The fire fighters came by asking for gasoline to burn them. You could see the genocidal Guardia coming in, with helicopters all over the place. We were sure our son had been over there, and was certainly one of those bodies. We went through anguish, uncertainty, for three days, and it was one of the greatest sufferings I've had in my whole life. But at the same time it was something marvelous, a pain that was bitter and yet very sweet. I don't know—I wouldn't know how to explain it and it's something that I still find moving when I recall it. And later finding out that they had managed to get out—how wonderful! It was like our child being born a second time.

—Is your Christian faith still the great moving force, the underlying motivation of your militancy in the revolution, when this process has enemies even in the church?

—You can see yourself, in everything I've been saying, there's always a cause of all causes and that's faith. I keep my faith commitment active. Naturally, it's not the kind of thing I think about all the time.

It goes without saying that any political project will make mistakes. But what is the purpose of politics? That's what the Somocistas and former politicians didn't understand. They thought it meant getting power and then taking it easy in the shade. For Christianity power is what Christ taught us: service. The least of the servants is the one who has the power. That's the way we think and that's the notion we have of politics. The very thing this people's revolutionary program is trying to do is to repair the injustice, to create a kingdom of love, not merely on an idealist or conceptual level, but to go about building it up day by day to make injustice gradually disappear. To reveal to the poor their poverty, to enable them to see that this situation of poverty must be changed, and to become involved in changing it, means filling the heart of the poor not with hatred but with hope. It simply means opening their eyes so they can get going on the way to liberation.

I go back to Managua after dark in a bus crowded with people, unbelievably overloaded. The things Zela has said, in our long and intense interview, stay with me.

13

HUMBERTO J. SOLIS

*President of the Appeals Court
in the Third Region*

**"I'm a man of the church, but I wouldn't be a good Christian if I
weren't involved in the process going on in my people"**

*Born in Boaco on August 20, 1932, Humberto José Solis studied law at the
National University of Nicaragua in León, receiving his doctorate in 1957. He
married Aurora Reyes Hernández in 1953 and they have four children and four*

grandchildren. Dr. Solis was a lawyer and notary public from 1958 to 1973. In 1968, after a Cursillo de Cristiandad, he left his law practice in order to work for the poor in the legal services agency at the UCA (Jesuit University) in Managua, and he directed that agency from 1973 to 1979. He was a Cursillo leader and took part in the effort at national pastoral planning in the early 1970s. From 1975 to 1979, he and his wife were involved in forming Christian communities in the rural parish of Comalapa (Prelature of Juigalpa). From 1979 to 1982 they were national coordinators of the Marriage Encounter and are still active in that movement. In 1979 Dr. Solis was made president of the High Labor Court and he is now presiding judge of the Appeals Court in Region III.

●

"From the Aguerri Theater, one block down" is the address of the High Labor Tribunal. That's the way addresses are in Nicaragua, like a spoken map, the names often changed and crossed out, as a result of the revolution.

I'm early for my appointment so I get a chance to look around at the ruins still left from the earthquake. I see Dr. Solis arrive in his Volkswagen but I wait until the specified time, contemplating the empty lots and open spaces down toward the lake where the ruins are cleaned up, some green areas and parks and the framework of some buildings, half-destroyed but still standing, occupied by families who have made homes in them. People here know a lot about earthquakes. They live on major faults and often feel tremors, especially at night.

I talk with Dr. Solis in his office. Sunlight filters in through the curtains. He has a New Testament, a crucifix, and other religious symbols and sayings on his desk and on the walls.

I gave up private practice as a lawyer in order to aid those who couldn't pay.

The first few phrases make me wonder whether his ancestors were German as do his hefty frame, high forehead, pinkish complexion, and hesitant, slow speech. Good-naturedly he corrects me: "My maternal last name is English. My grandfather on my mother's side was English. Everyone knows me as just Pepe Solis.

Q—What was your work before the revolutionary victory?

*Solis—*At first I worked in the private sector as part of a prestigious law firm here in Nicaragua and as a company lawyer. Later, during a process of Christian conversion I came to a point in my life when I questioned what I was doing with my professional services.

When the 1972 earthquake hit, that questioning increased, because the companies our firm worked for were taking advantage of the people's misery by "legally" pillaging their houses and property. At that point I gave up exercising my profession in the private sector. The Catholic University offered me the job of heading the Legal Services Office, which provided legal advice and aid for those who couldn't pay. My income went way down, but it was a great experience for my Christian life, one that was enormously enriching. I was involved in that apostolate for seven years when I was called by the revolution to take charge of this delicate responsibility in November 1979.

—You've suggested that you're a Christian. How long has that been? All your life, or from a particular moment? You've said you experienced a conversion at a particular point. What was your early education like?

—I was born into a Christian family. My father had great faith. My mother did too, but it was especially true of my father. I used to see that he had a great faith in God, in God's providence. I had a traditional sort of education: believing in God and what I learned in school, Catholic school, memorizing gospel passages, things like that. The only thing special I can recall from that time was that, when I was little, I used to serve Mass for the pastor and go along with him when he went out on missions to the outlying towns in Boaco.

When I was fifteen I came to Managua with my family. I was young, twenty-one, when I married Aurora Reyes from León, who was sixteen. We have four children (twin daughters and two sons), all of them married now. At this point we're raising grandchildren.

My faith was quite routine all during my adolescence and youth. On a personal level, my married life was very up-and-down, all messed up. Sure, I always kept up certain practices, like going to Mass, and wanting my children to go to Mass, things like that. But there came a point when I was even dropping these things and then I gave up religious practices completely. That was true until 1968, when I had been married for fifteen years, and I was invited to a Cursillo de Christiandad. It was there that a change in my life took place. In the cursillo I saw quite clearly what the message of Christianity was and what faith commitment it required: it was not a matter of forms but of life. At that point I began to want to change, to sincerely seek change. I questioned myself more and more, and I became more and more involved in the church's structures. I was involved in pastoral work, in preparing the effort at organized pastoral work that was attempted in 1972, and then in the Pastoral Week organized in the archdiocese of Managua. I worked on the archdiocesan coordinating team. All during this period I kept asking myself how I could live my faith alongside the poor. This dilemna had thrown me into great turmoil when I was a lawyer for several exploitative companies and yet wanted to live a Christian life. I also worked in different church movements, in the grassroots

Christian communities in the parish of Santa Ana, which was my own parish at that time. From 1974 until the revolutionary victory, both my wife and I were in charge of a rural parish in Chontales where there was no priest, no pastor. That's the parish of Comalapa. The bishop of Chontales asked us to work there at evangelization and at forming peasant Christian communities.

—How did you carry out that work of evangelization? What kind of results did you get?

—Once we were invited to Comalapa to give a retreat. The way the peasants there were exploited and living in utter poverty hit us hard. From that time on we began to figure out how we could dedicate our activity, at least on weekends, to an evangelization that would be consciousness-raising. Besides the material misery of the people there, their spiritual misery was so great, their faith so naive and so passive that the peasants thought their terrible situation of poverty was God's will. As we went on, we discovered that if there was to be a true liberation in our country, the first thing we'd have to do would be to lead the poorest, the most outcast and abandoned, to become aware of their human situation and their dignity as God's children.

We were involved in this experience for five years, from 1974 to 1979. We used to go out on Friday evening and come back Sunday night. We visited all the districts in the area, and even carried out some pastoral activity on the prelature level. We were able to form Christian communities in several districts. We went by jeep, horseback, and on foot. Sometimes priests from here, from Managua, especially Jesuits, went along with us. We took them whenever we thought it would be a good idea to celebrate the sacraments. We received more than we gave, both my wife and I. It was also good for the Christian formation of our children, our example of involvement in this pastoral work of consciousness-raising evangelization among the peasants. Now the communities are moving along on their own and participating in the revolution. This is the richest Christian experience we've had.

I became disenchanted with traditional political parties, and I discovered Christ as the way to complete salvation.

—When and how did you begin to take part in the anti-Somoza struggle?

—To some extent, I began when I was a child, since my father was in the opposition. He belonged to the Conservative Party and was never involved in "pacts" [the deals Somoza made with his political opposition] and always rejected them. I grew up in that same spirit. I took part in university struggles against the Somoza system. Then, during my professional career, I belonged to the Conservative Party, and was in an active cadre. In 1967 there was an election, a complete fraud like all of them, and then Agüero's betrayal, when he joined the Senate and so became an accomplice to all the fraud.* That was why I became disenchanted with political parties and broke with them. When I began my conversion I could see that the political maneuvering of political parties would not save our people, but that only a real process of consciousness-raising could bring that about.

From that time on I've stayed away from active party politics, and I've been involved in church movements, church structures, in order to work along the lines I've mentioned, with a concern for the common good, for what will benefit those who are poorest.

—*How did you, both of you, you and your wife, take part in the final insurrection against Somoza?*

—All my involvement in the struggle and my wife's also remained within the bounds of active nonviolence. Because of our Christian formation, violence was a problem for us. I came to the point where I thought that under no circumstances could a Christian accept violence, not even by way of exception. I even doubted the church's teaching recognizing the legitimacy of violence as an exceptional case. I read Helder Camara, Gandhi, and Martin Luther King, and I thought that peaceful methods, nonviolent methods, for defeating the Somoza regime had not been exhausted. That's why I wasn't involved in armed struggle in any way, even though some of my children were. That created conflict in the family. But when they murdered Pedro Joaquín Chamorro and the people's indignation burst loose, and when the people were brutally and savagely repressed by the dictatorship, which went so far as to bomb cities and neighborhoods, I became convinced that the church was wise in teaching that violence is a legitimate last recourse against a prolonged tyranny. Even the bishops recognized the legitimacy of the insurrection in their pastoral letter.

During the final insurrection I went to join with the Red Cross, and saw the suffering and despair of the people as they left their poor barrios seeking refuge from the bombing. I took charge of coordinating the refugee centers that were set up in Managua.

—*Throughout your life what has been your notion of Sandino and his ideas?*

—What I knew about Sandino was mainly the evil that was said of him. I had never read the true story of his life, and I was unaware of his ideas. I got my information only from the traditional parties. There came a moment when I saw him as a patriot, as someone who had struggled like many other people. I never fully comprehended Sandino until after the revolutionary victory and I began to study his ideas, his life, everything. I now regret I didn't do that earlier. I keep on studying him and I admire him more and more. It's something

---

*At a time of political difficulties, Somoza offered a share in power to his old rival and leader of the Conservative Party, Fernando Argüero. Argüero's "betrayal" was denounced by many Conservatives, Social Christians, and Liberals.—ED.

like what happened when I began to get to know Christ, his life, his gospel—I regretted not having known him before. Of course you have to keep in mind the proper distinctions and the substantial distance between them. In no way do I identify Sandino with Jesus Christ; I don't even compare them. This connection between my own experiences has occurred to me now, but I make the proper distinction between them.

—*What is your Christian life like today, in the midst of the revolutionary process?*

—I had some doubts when I was called to take this position, since in Legal Services I felt fulfilled in my commitment to the poor and in my Christian life. I checked with friends, with priests, and even with the rector of the UCA (Jesuit University) and they helped me see that this work could provide better services for poor people all over Nicaragua, for those who are part of the labor force, and that means most of our people. So my Christian faith is nourished by my striving to make each judicial sentence, each step I take, each thing I study, each letter I write, aim toward justice for the poor, something that has been treated with so much contempt, something that has been missing in Nicaragua for so long.

In order to strengthen my faith and avoid the danger of being reduced to sheer activism, I remain involved in a group of Christian reflection, Christians in the Revolution. My wife and I also work in the Marriage Encounter. We are convinced that the formation of the new society has to take hold in the family. The family is the foundation, and you have to take care of it. We believe the rebuilding of Nicaragua has to be political, economic, and social, of course, but it also has to be moral and spiritual—and perhaps that should be first. On this point, we think the family should play a very important role, since any new building has to sit on a firm foundation, right? And if the family falls apart, who knows where we could begin to build up a new society the way we would like it?

—*Does this revolutionary process offer enough real possibilities for spiritually rebuilding the nation, individuals, and the family?*

—The revolution doesn't operate against the family. So many families have broken up in the thick of revolutionary activity, but I think that's because there wasn't any true work done to strengthen the family before this.

—*What kinds of prayer do you practice now?*

—The same kind of individual personal prayer as before, when I would kneel in the presence of the Blessed Sacrament for prayer and meditation. I don't have time to do it that way with the work I have in this position. But you can see I've got my New Testament right here. I'd say my prayer is now more connected with life. With each step, each decision I make, each thing I write, I turn to God and ask for light, since in labor matters you have to make decisions based on conscience and not so much on the letter of the law. I ask God to enlighten my conscience so all my decisions will be connected to true justice and will favor the poor.

My wife and I together keep up a kind of family prayer. We keep up our prayer as a marriage and that gives us strength. And then there is prayer in Christian groups. I'm involved in what we call Christians in the Revolution. I'm one of the founders of this movement. In groups we reflect on our participation in the revolution in the light of our faith.

Besides that, my wife and I belong to the Marriage Encounter. We've just finished three years as national coordinators, and we continue to participate, giving weekend retreats to twenty-five or thirty couples. So that's somewhere else that we put our faith to work, and deepen it, and pray.

—*I can see that Christianity is very much a part of both of you, and that you are very attached to the church and also quite identified with the revolution. Don't you run into obstacles and contradictions that way?*

—Being decisively and fully involved in the life of the church has been a part of me. Both in communities and in movements, I've always worked with the bishops and enjoyed good relations with them.

I couldn't consider myself a Christian, really living a Christian life, unless I were a part of this revolutionary process of my people. I'm more convinced of this every day. Every day I see more clearly that this revolutionary project is going in a direction that will benefit those who are poorest, the vast majority. And I believe my faith, the gospel, Christ's message, is just that, the overall liberation of those who have been most cast aside, the poorest, the weakest. That's where I find strong, basic convergence.

—*What is your prediction for the future?*

—Well, being as realistic and objective as I can, the least I can say is that the future of Christianity in Nicaragua is going to demand a lot more purifying.

Since the moment of revolutionary victory, I've been saying that now it's more difficult to be a Christian than before, since we Christians are now called to a challenge and a commitment that is much greater than it was before. It used to be enough to give up something extra, some luxury, and you felt like a good Christian. But now we see so many people who don't claim to be Christian giving up their time, their property, their life, everything. We have a much greater challenge, and we have to give a witness that is much greater and much more difficult. It's my hope that the sector identified with the process will grow all the time. But, being realistic, I think we're going to get to a situation here of Christianity in small communities, a minority Christianity, called to be ferment, to be leaven, to be salt within this process. What I see is that the split in the church is going to become more pronounced, the church is going to become more divided. And that makes me sad.

—*What are the likely consequences for coming generations? How do you see present and future Christianity for the youth of Nicaragua?*

—Young people are going to get to the point—if they're not already there— of rejecting the present structures of our church, which they see as identified with those positions that are most reactionary toward our process. That poses a great challenge for those of us who are Christians. I think our witness, our commitment, our living of an authentic and real faith, is the only thing that can lead the young people of Nicaragua to feel any attraction toward the Christian faith.

—*What are, or what should be, the contributions Christians make to the revolution?*

—The Christian new person has to be much purer, much more committed, much more radical in every way than before. But we have to be careful not to fall into striving for the sake of appearance, or presuming that we are better persons than revolutionaries who don't claim to be Christians. We should even humbly recognize that we make our mistakes, and that in the revolution we are all seeking a common goal, which is happiness for everyone. We can make a distinction on the basis of the eschatological dimension of our faith, but we can't separate ourselves from the rest in the work of improving the living conditions of our people nor should we insist that others be like us. We shouldn't be fanatic and intolerant. Let's be authentic on our side, and let them be authentic on theirs, because authenticity comes only from living up to what you say you believe and that's what counts.

Weeks later, I'm prompted by Pepe Solis's charism involving him in the church to go back to get his impression on the pope's visit to Nicaragua. Without losing his almost clerical composure and tone, he says:

It was very painful. Regrettable. No one could have wanted things to happen the way they did. I hoped that when he talked it would be his heart speaking and not the bad information some people had given him. But it was not him speaking. He didn't take our real situation into account. As for the people's reaction at the celebration of the Eucharist, I don't approve of it and can't approve of it. But I understand it, looking at it from the viewpoint of the grief of those who, two days earlier, had buried those seventeen young people who had been killed by armed counterrevolutionaries. With their wounds still fresh, those people were waiting for the pope to offer them a word of hope.

14

MIGUEL ERNESTO VIJIL

Minister of Housing and Human Settlements

"It is following Jesus Christ that makes it obligatory for me to take part in this revolution"

Miguel Ernesto Vijil was born in Managua on October 19, 1937. In 1963 he married Pina Gurdián; they have six children. From 1961 to 1965 he was an engineer with Elvir Herdocia Construction Engineers. He then directed the office of planning of the National University (1965-1971). From 1972 to 1979 he was assistant manager of Gurdián S.A. y Compañias Afiliadas, dealing in agricultural equipment and supplies. Vigil's anti-Somoza activity developed gradually, an outgrowth of his traditional Catholic education. Together with his wife, he has been active in apostolic movements in the Catholic Church. Since July 20, 1979, he has been the Minister of Housing and Human Settlements. He was a member of official missions the Nicaraguan government sent to the Vatican between 1980 and 1982.

●

The Ministry of Housing and Human Settlements is near the Claretian community of Las Palmas, where I live, so I've walked there under a fiercely hot gray sky. A surprisingly strong summer gust raises clouds of dust that mix with the smoke coming from the dry grass people are burning on the empty lots in the barrios of Managua. The Ministry is set in the midst of an experimental project of low-cost housing.

At 5:30, his work day over, Miguel Ernesto answers my questions in a silence that is broken only by the buzz of the air conditioner. This office, small, closed-in, and windowless, with wood-paneling, carpets, and heavy furniture, would suffocate us if we didn't have this source of cool air.

> **Within the revolutionary process I'm growing in my awareness of the gospel mandate to follow Jesus Christ.**

Vijil—I'm fully involved in this revolutionary process. Besides working as Minister of Housing and Human Settlements, I'm also a member of the Sandinista National Liberation Front. I'm involved in many activities: I take part in activities the revolution promotes, such as voluntary work, the people's militia, and other things that come up, insofar as my responsibilities allow.

Q—How do you live your Christian faith in the midst of this complete dedication to the revolution?

—First I should tell you in all sincerity that my Christian faith has never been more alive. Today my Christian faith is firmer and more solid than ever—a faith based on a deep commitment to Christ, with an ever-growing understanding of the gospel mandate to imitate or follow Jesus Christ as a model with whom I should identify in my life. That leads me to be part of Christians in the Revolution and to take part in Christian meetings, celebrations, and activities.

To be honest, I have to point out that my liturgical practice has gone down. I don't take part in liturgies as much as I would like—for several reasons. The main reason is not overwork and lack of time, but the sad fact that now in

Managua it's not easy to have access to services and preaching in tune with the way those of us who are revolutionaries are living our faith. But I keep trying to maintain some connection with the Christian community as it meets to pray and to express its faith in the Eucharist.

I'm aware of Miguel Ernesto's concerns because we've often been together in prayer and reflection on the faith during liturgical celebrations and Christian meetings. He's a regular participant in meetings, retreats, and days of reflection, and he takes part with spontaneity, he enters into things, he always has something to contribute. I asked him to recount his participation in the different stages and forms of the struggle against the Somoza regime.

—When I was a high-school student in Nicaragua between 1950 and 1955, I was deeply opposed to the Somoza government because of the notorious abuses of the regime, administrative corruption, one-man despotic rule, the use of power for personal benefit, and the National Guard's cruel repression of the people—all the injustices that were so well known. At that time I didn't question the structural injustices of the system. My concern was that there be a new political regime in Nicaragua, and I didn't get into questioning the economic system and the social system.

Within the limitations present in Nicaragua, I took a modest part in some of the activities of opposition to the regime at that time. Then I went away to study in the United States. I studied civil engineering at the Catholic University in Washington from 1955 to 1959. During my last year there, revolutionary movements were taking place in Latin America, and they had a strong impact in my country. It all happened around the time of the Cuban revolution (1959). Right away hopes were raised in Nicaragua, movements sprang up with a revolutionary spirit, and I became involved in those movements. I was twenty-one years old and my political ideas had changed a lot. From a conservative position, I had moved along toward a kind of socialism of a social democratic sort.

> **All I knew about Marxism was what I had learned in school through the traditional apologetics against Marxism.**

—Involved in the struggles of opposition political parties, I was searching for a way in which Nicaragua could change, not only in its government, but also in its structures. I recall that in my mind I was working out sketches of what a new structure could be. But I bypassed the tools for analyzing society scientifically since at that time I didn't know anything about them. All I knew about Marxism was what we had learned in our last years in high school through the traditional apologetics against Marxism. That was what they taught in Catholic schools at that time, an apologetics aimed at avoiding and combating what were regarded as the errors of Marxism. We studied Marxism in order to combat it and to prove that it was false and contrary to the spirit of Christianity. All through this period, I fiercely maintained my traditional religious ideas.

The day after I graduated, in June 1959, I went to Cuba to join a movement that was beginning, a continuation of Olama y Mollejones (an attempt at an armed coup to overthrow Somoza). It was all under the umbrella of a coalition of political parties in Nicaragua called the Nicaraguan Revolutionary Movement. Its leader was Dr. Lacayo Farfán, and among his chief advisors were Pedro Joaquín Chamorro and others who would appear in subsequent developments in Nicaragua. When that invasion failed and the National Guard destroyed everything, we couldn't leave Cuba, and so we were up in the air. However, the Nicaraguan Revolutionary Movement continued and I stayed on in Cuba, working with it.

I'd like to mention that while I was in Cuba, I had the chance to get to know Carlos Fonseca, and was with him several times. He was a person on fire with a mission. At that time we didn't mesh very well, since Carlos's stance was already clearly one of struggling against the social and economic structures of Nicaragua, and I hadn't yet broken away from them. That's the way it was. Nevertheless we did see each other and relate to each other.

Things got worse in Nicaragua. The government got stronger, and chances for doing anything were reduced more and more. Under a general amnesty I returned to the country in May 1960. Since I wanted to continue studying, to go into law, I enrolled as a student at the National University in León. I moved to León and stayed there for almost twenty years.

That year, 1960, I helped groups who were active in the university. I took part in different actions such as the first university takeover. I was also involved in activities connected with the attack on the army garrisons in Jinotepe and Diriamba in November 1960.

In December of that year, my life underwent a big change. Since I had to make a living, I helped set up a construction company, and I'm a shareholder in it to this day. I went to work full-time and that took me away from other activities, but I still was concerned about the university struggle and I used to spend a lot of time there. Although I was working in the private sector, I also continued to be a student. I took law courses, studied part-time, and kept up with movements in the university. When Carlos Tünnermann became rector, he asked me to join his staff as director of the office of planning.

From 1960 on, I was an active member of the Independent Liberal Party and held positions in it until 1969, when I left it. By then, political activity had become a burden to me, since I had undergone a deep internal change in 1966, one that affected the rhythm and direction of my life.

During my time in the university my political ideas were moving more and more in the direction of socialism. In the university I was in contact with people who had very clear ideas about politics. We talked things over a lot, and I became more and more convinced that the social structure of Nicaragua had to be changed. In 1969 I handed in my letter of resignation to the Independent Liberal Party, leaving everything in order. I no longer played an active role in political organizations, but I took part in isolated actions, demonstrations, and meetings, and I always gave money and support to political activities in the province of León.

—What happened in your life in 1966? What was the change that took place? Did it affect your Christianity, your professional life, or your political awareness?

—It affected everything. It was a deep religious change. With all my traditional, conservative religious baggage, the way I had been focused on orthodoxy and on religious practice since my childhood out of fear of God and the fear of hell, I was invited to participate in a Cursillo de Cristiandad. I went and took part. And there, in that cursillo, there began a deep change in the way I saw religion. I began to discover Christianity. I began to see the Lord as a model to follow. And I discovered that love rather than fear could be the motivating force in my activity. Naturally that transformation didn't happen overnight. It was a process that gradually deepened.

The more I became convinced of the need to be an authentic Christian, the further I moved away from my social group. I experienced a Christian conversion, and that led me to break away from my social class—it was both logical and clear-cut. This break took place in practice, without my looking for theories or ideologies. It took place in habits and daily actions, in life.

I'll give an example. In León, a city that is small and traditional and where social divisions are sharply defined, a party was always held at the Club on New Year's Eve—it was the high point in the city's social life. At that party the young women of the leading families in the city made their debut. Those who took part were the cream, the flower, of society in León. Since it is a small city, some families walked to the party, men in their formal suits and women in elegant long dresses. In the street, the underprivileged, the poor, lined up to see these people of the aristocracy; the poor crowded around the door to watch the rich go in to the party. One day, talking this over in our family and with a group of friends, we remarked that this couldn't be in harmony with a Christian life, since Christianity unites people and makes them brothers and sisters, while this kind of society party divides them. The division is an offense to those who can't go, who are left to watch the privileged stroll by and go in. My wife and I decided not to go to the party and instead we arranged for a Mass to be said. A Mass is still celebrated on New Year's Eve at the Church of the Recollection in León. Instead of going to the party at the Club, after the Mass all the cursillistas from every social class, poor, rich, everyone—we used to go to a friend's house, in our shirtsleeves. That was a symbolic gesture of breaking away that caused quite a stir—such a stir that those who continued to go to the party at the Club harbored resentment against us. The bad feeling and personal enmity toward my wife and me that began then still exists. Many people who are no longer even in Nicaragua, who are in Miami, consider us traitors.

Christian faith led me to more and more radical commitments and political actions against Somoza and his regime.

As time went on, the split grew deeper. I became more and more identified with the dispossessed, the outcast, the poorest. It wasn't easy or comfortable to do that. People didn't approve. They saw us as eccentrics, or as insulting them. But the real problem was our growing commitment to the poor. More and more that was cutting us off from high society in León and putting us at odds with them. This same Christian commitment led us to take part in political protests, actions of taking churches and defending political prisoners. My wife and I took part in this in different ways—by giving money, lending our car, fixing food and taking it to those who had taken over a church, things that were quite risky and dangerous at that time.

In 1977 with the taking of San Carlos, Ocotal, and Masaya, the struggle leaped forward. It was the beginning of insurrectionary struggle. The group of the Twelve came forward, and there was a series of public statements: I signed some, drafted several, and collected signatures in León. The need to be involved in political action and to support the struggle became greater and reached a high point with the murder of Pedro Joaquín Chamorro on January 10, 1978. Right away we had to organize something and get a general strike going. I was one of the members of the strike committee in León. We didn't think Somoza would be able to withstand an extended general strike. In fact he did hold on. We were on strike for two weeks. Since 1972 I had been working in a company in the private sector, and we were quite well off economically. I was assistant manager and had a great deal of administrative responsibility in that company, which was the biggest in León and one of the biggest in the country. Despite all that, we took part in the work stoppage. We were the first to shut down and join the strike, and we organized the progressive part of the private sector in the city to join the strike. We set out to organize and to forge an alliance of all forces in the country, including the Sandinista National Liberation Front.

Then the uprising of September 1978 took place, and the situation in the country became chaotic. Some of the officials in the company where I worked fled the country. That left a heavier burden of administration on those of us who remained. The insurrection took place during the time of year when the fumigation of the cotton crop was going on. Our company was hit hard financially. I continued to work along with the revolutionary struggle. From the moment the Twelve set foot in Nicaragua, I was involved in helping them. That was in July 1978. My house was their meeting place in León.

In Nicaragua the time has come to do something about imitating and following Jesus in poverty and sacrifice on behalf of those who are poorest.

From the time of victory I've worked in the revolution in the field of housing. I've put my whole self into it. Obviously we've made mistakes, but we've gone forward. Our rate of housing construction during these three years has been higher than Somoza's throughout his whole time in power, including the periods of peace and prosperity, with all the economic possibilities he had. We have to work with all kinds of problems and our resources are very limited, but we've thrown our whole selves into this work and we've taken revolutionary measures regarding land and housing on behalf of the neediest.

— *That the majority of the people in Managua need decent human housing is obvious, painfully obvious. The revolution opens one's eyes to how great the needs in these countries are, how deeply wounded they are.*

— The housing needs left behind by the Somoza system (and aggravated by the earthquake and the war) are so great that we aren't able to solve them as efficiently and quickly as we might like. We've been able to work out the theory of how the problems should be solved, to carry out some practical actions immediately, and to set up an instrument, the Ministry of Housing, which can put into effect whatever measures the revolutionary government judges necessary. Within the ministry we've been able to create a climate of working together as a team. We first did some thinking about what had to be done, and now we're doing it.

With this revolutionary process, the time has come when we can, and we must, make the Christian commitment to imitate and follow Jesus Christ in something practical and real, in poverty and sacrifice on behalf of the majority, those who have always been poor, oppressed, and cast aside. It is putting Christian love into practice.

— *Several times you've said that your previous education and your Christian mindset kept you from knowing about and using the Marxist method for scientifically analyzing reality. Have you changed in that regard?*

— I'm going to take a bit of time to tell you about my personal experience in that regard, since I came around to seeing and experiencing how true it was what Karl Marx said: that it is the sweat of the workers that builds up capital. This is how I arrived at that viewpoint through personal experience.

One year had been especially good for our company finances. For our annual meeting I was asked to pull together information on how much the company's capital had increased from the beginning up to that year, which was 1976, I believe. The idea was to see how much the value of what the shareholders had initially payed had multiplied above and beyond the dividends they had received, which I was also going to calculate. I drew up a chart showing the dividends received each year plus the increase in the amount of capital the company had built up by that year. And I added it all up. The amount was really extraordinary and showed that the economic performance had been very profitable for the shareholders. The capital had multiplied several times. That chart stayed in my mind. I left the chart on my desk and went home for lunch.

When I came back in the afternoon, I began to ask myself where all this money had come from, how it was possible that the money had multiplied so. And one thing was quite clear to me: the stockholders hadn't produced it. Many of them had never set foot in the plant except for the annual meeting. They had never contributed anything more than their modest initial payment. Hence it was clear that this huge growth in money had not been produced by their activity. My first reaction was to think that it was the administrators of the company, including myself, who had produced the money, and so that money should be ours. But I quickly realized that that wasn't true, since the company paid its administrators very well. I only have to tell you that at that time the income tax I paid—and it wasn't as much as I should have paid legally—was more than my present annual salary as Minister of Housing and Human Settlements.

So it was clear that we administrators weren't the ones being impoverished by the way capital was piling up, since we were all well paid. So I came to the conclusion that the company's workers were being exploited, but I was wrong again, since the workers in that company got good wages. They're still better paid than workers in the other companies I know about. And besides getting good wages, they had a whole series of benefits: the company paid for medicine and medical treatment for the worker, his wife, and their children, and besides that, it paid for school expenses, textbooks, bonuses, and other kinds of help that were really unprecedented in Nicaragua. The company gave its workers a lot of very good benefits—in a paternalistic way, of course.

Doing a little figuring to see how the overall wealth of all Nicaraguans could be distributed, I could see that these workers were, and to this day still are, paid far more than the average that would be coming to each Nicaraguan in justice and in accordance with the gross national product. Consequently, it must not be they who were being impoverished by this process. So I had to consider another group, the customers, those who bought the company's agricultural supplies, especially for cotton farming. I ran down the list of customers in my mind, since I knew them quite well. Each of them had made a lot of money growing cotton. They had nice houses, made trips to other countries, owned cars, gave big parties, could afford drinks at the Club, and so forth. And so I was forced to come down to the Nicaraguan peasant, the one who picked the cotton, who planted it, and took care of it, the one who sweated. It was the peasant masses of Nicaragua, who with their sweat and effort were producing the money for others to have an easy life and to keep piling up profits to the point that the shareholders' accumulated capital was reproducing itself.

That's how I came to learn the scientific method for analyzing reality in order to uncover the mechanisms of exploitation, then to search for a way to combat it, and in so doing to better carry out the gospel mandate. All this is consistent with the gospel message that my life must be centered on serving the rest—my life can't be for myself.

> **For me it would be more comfortable to go on living the way I used to instead of living this commitment to the revolution, which means becoming poor and undergoing painful breaks with the past.**

—Has your Christian faith gone through other changes or breaks with the past through your experience in revolutionary struggle?

—Now I feel better able to understand how to make the gospel commandment to love one another something real here in Nicaragua, today, and in what's left of this century. I've come to understand that there are different ways to express love, according to the time, the place, and who it is you love. The love you show toward the people, the people as a whole, is expressed in a commitment to improve the structures that can then better the living conditions of that people. This brings us to a point that I regard as all-embracing, namely, that political activity is not something outside Christian life. Political activity is a duty of Christianity, a demand of the Christian faith, because, correctly understood, politics means carrying out the commitment you have to love this group made up of all those who live within the territory of Nicaragua, to love all your brothers and sisters in the community of the nation.

—How has the revolution forced you to be more Christian? Can you illustrate that with concrete cases?

—For example, one of the commandments we have as Christians is to strive toward a poverty that is generous—not the poverty of depriving ourselves of necessary possessions, but an austerity in one's person, family, and community, so as to serve the whole population, to share, so that everyone may have those goods that are necessary, and the whole structural system may work to assure that. Well, the revolutionary process makes it easy for me, even forces me, to live this Christian commandment realistically. I now consciously accept the fact that my life is, and is going to be, poorer in what I own. This is contrary to what I had always considered the economic ideal for the family, that each year should be better. I know that each year is going to be worse, that each year I'm going to have fewer things. What we've saved is going to be used up, inflation is going to erode what I earn, and my own finances are going to become more precarious every day. I accept that consciously, as living out my Christian mission in life.

Along with that, as part of the same Christian message, I know that my service should become more and more efficient. I should work more and I should be sharper at my work. I should be working now with the same ability I used in the private sector to make money for the owners of the company and for myself. I regard that as a religious duty, as the Christian duty of commitment to others.

My life has now been brought together, made whole. It's no longer a question of a job on one side, religion somewhere else, and a family somewhere else. All aspects are interrelated: my family life, my religious life, my work life. It's all one thing, everything is blended together. These are facets of one reality, one life; there is an overall process of inner integration, and that has given me an enormous spiritual peace in the midst of a lot of work, a huge amount of work.

This confession of Miguel Ernesto's has a ring of sincerity, and it demands a moment of silence in the interview. It is a moment of intense communication, of a contagious peacefulness.

—*How do you explain the warnings, the fears, and even the attitudes of excommunication expressed by some groups of Christians, clergy, and hierarchy against the revolutionary process and against Christians who participate in it?*

—They're trying to maintain and justify, with an appearance of Christianity, a situation and a system that sustains a privileged minority. For example, I just listened to a speech made at a professional meeting in which one of the officers said that in 1981 more than one hundred engineers had left Nicaragua, and that they had left to look for work where their efforts would be rewarded more justly. He said that the revolutionary government's maximum salary of 10,000 córdobas [US $1,000 at the official exchange rate and around US $350 at the parallel rate—TRANS.] is unjust, that they deserve more. On what basis can someone claim a higher salary in a poor country, when the working class doesn't even get paid 1,000 córdobas a month? When people claim to be concerned about religion and to be afraid of what will happen to religion, what's really involved when you get down to it, is an economic and social problem. They don't want to accept the fact that we will have to become poor so that the majority can rise out of the misery and exploitation they've lived in for their whole lives.

I sincerely believe that underlying all this is a conflict over power. Many people are unwilling to accept the fact that what's going on here in Nicaragua is a revolution, that this revolution was led by the Sandinista National Liberation Front, and that at this point the Sandinista Front is the leading force in this country. That's the fact they aren't willing to accept. Why? Because the Sandinistas are young people, many of them from humble origins. Because they aren't the kind of people that many have gotten used to seeing in high positions for four hundred years in this country. But that's not a good reason to oppose it. In fact, the domination by corrupt politicians and sold-out rulers for these past four centuries has made it necessary for people from the humble and exploited class to come and change things.

The plain fact is that the members of the Sandinista Front led the revolution and are in power because they earned it. And it is a fact that they are exercising that power in favor of the majority. That doesn't mean that no mistakes are made. I have made mistakes as Minister of Housing. That can happen to anyone in any government, especially anyone who has to begin in a new field, starting from scratch, surrounded by vast needs and a huge backload of inherited problems. That's what happened here. The revolutionary government now wants to clean this all up and to put the country's resources at the service of the majority of the people in a revolutionary way. There are people in Nicaragua who have the experience and know-how to do this job, but they don't want to because the State pays them too little. So others who are willing to work in a revolutionary spirit are appointed, but they don't have the professional experience and they make mistakes. Mistakes, not abuses. And those who could do the work better, but don't want to, point out the mistakes and blow them out of proportion, and they, along with other people, then make accusations and even calumniate, since they portray exceptions as though they were the rule. What do they want? What they want is that the state not be revolutionary, but go back to what it was before, and that the Club, with its society debuts and all the rest, continue to exist. That's what they want.

> I think the specific contribution Christians make to the revolution is their motivation, which comes from faith in the God of Jesus Christ, for whom they commit themselves to his people.

—Do Christians have something to contribute to the revolution, some particular thing that comes from their identity as Christians?

—I don't see any reason to make a distinction between the activities of a revolutionary who is a Christian and a revolutionary who doesn't regard himself or herself as a Christian. There can't be any distinction in revolutionary actions. Distinctions would appear in other things.

I think the proper and specific characteristic of Christians in the revolution is their motivation by faith in God, faith in Jesus Christ, their deep personal motivation to be committed to the people, to all one's brothers and sisters.

Those of us who are Christians and are involved in this revolution need to pause on the road for reflection and prayer, depending on one's pace and the particular groups one may be part of. It's something like going out to the desert to pray. We need times or moments for meditation in order to get back on the road so that our interior life can keep pace with our experience. In this sense, the hierarchy, priests and religious, some of them could and should have an enormous contribution to make, and no one's doing it now: no one is providing the means, the way to carry out this kind of reflection, this kind of meditation. Someone would have to discover, create, or start for Christian revolutionaries at the end of the twentieth century what St. Ignatius did for people in his time with the Spiritual Exercises.

We've been conversing for over two hours without a break, without even having anything to drink. True, the air conditioning has protected us from the suffocating heat, but the time has come to end the interview. I wrap it up in the conventional way—"Do you want to add anything more?"—quite sure that he won't add anything after being subjected to so many questions and after giving such thorough answers. But to my surprise Miguel Ernesto takes the small tape recorder in his hands:

—Yes I do want to add something else to what we've said.

Because of the way you've put things and the questions you've asked, I've emphasized the positive aspects of my life. I haven't had the chance to speak about the negative aspects. I don't think this is the proper time, since this isn't a confession. Nevertheless, my life has never at any time been one of full commitment. I'd like to finish our conversation by noting my failures, because I know I'm a sinful man.

I'm thinking that somehow in this area there may be a specifically Christian contribution to the revolution: not being triumphalistic, not being someone who thinks he or she owns the truth and has all the answers, but knowing that you're a sinner, and that despite your sin and your weakness you're moving ahead because you feel impelled to struggle for your brothers and sisters. A deep religious conviction moves you to be fully aware that in this struggle, and at the end of this struggle, in some mysterious way—I don't know how—you're going to meet the Lord, who is waiting for you with open arms. But the way to this Lord, the way to this goal, must of necessity pass through commitment to your brothers and sisters, to the poorest, to those who are most in need. With a full awareness of my sins, I feel more alive than ever in my life of faith, as I serve this revolutionary people.

Afterward Miguel Ernesto takes me to his house in the Eduardo Contreras Barrio. I meet Pinita, his wife, and most of his children, Miguel Ernesto, 17, Virginia, 16, Félix, 14, Francisco, 11, and Ana Margarita, 5. They've all chosen to become involved in the people's revolution and are doing revolutionary work. Missing is Josefina, the oldest, 19, who is in the hills with the Omar Torrijos Brigade, defending the revolution against armed attackers.

We talk and eat supper, and they give me some clippings of articles Miguel Ernesto and Pina have written about Christianity within the revolution and copies of some prayers.

Several months later I recall Miguel Ernesto's home, and that helps me understand a long poem of his published in Ventana *("This Is My House") in which he mentions his wife, his children, and a good friend of the family. At the end of the poem he prays "May God bless this house of ours/a house ready for war and bristling with guns/but like all Nicaragua, yearning to live in peace and in love."*

GLOSSARY OF TERMS

Barricada. Nicaragua's newspaper of the ideological left.

Christians in the Revolution. A group of Nicaraguan Christians who support one another in their commitment to the revolution and to the Christian faith. Many of them are in the Nicaraguan government.

Compañeros. Members of the Sandinista Front.

Cordoba. Nicaraguan unit of currency. Official rate of exchange: 10,000 = U.S. $1,000.

Contras. Counterrevolutionary forces.

Council of State. Nicaragua's legislative body: 33 seats are divided between traditional political parties or organizations dominated by the bourgeoisie and members of the Front; 14 seats are held by members of mass organizations such as teachers, workers, clergy.

Insurrection. A nationwide but premature attempt to overthrow Somoza led by the FSLN in September 1978. It was crushed by the National Guard.

Insurrectionists. See *Terceristas.*

Land Reform. Principles put into effect shortly after victory. Right to ownership of land is based on productive and efficient use rather than size.

Muchachos. Young people of the Sandinista Front.

National Guard. Nicaragua's standing army before 1979; considered by many to be in effect the Somoza family's personal bodyguard.

El Nuevo Diario. Nicaragua's newspaper of the religious left.

La Prensa. Nicaragua's newspaper of the ideological and religious right.

National Assembly. Legislative body and constituent assembly set up with 1984 elections. Its major task is to draw up a new constitution within two years.

Proletariat. Tendency that emerged out of the FSLN during the 1970s favoring building a strong political base in urban areas over rural guerrilla tactics.

Sandinismo. Term used to describe Nicaragua's current philosophy. It is described as resting on four pillars: nationalism, democratic participation, gospel values, and social justice.

Somocismo. Term used to describe system of corruption and exploitation as experienced during the regime of the Somoza family.

Terceristas. Tendency that emerged out of the FSLN during the 1970s; favored building a strong military organization to attack Somoza's forces from outside Nicaragua over mass organizing within the country.

The Twelve. Influential Nicaraguan businessmen, clergy, and intellectuals, a creation of the *Terceristas* rather than the bourgeoisie. When they returned from exile in Costa Rica in July 1978 they called for the constitution of a popular government with FSLN participation.

Other Orbis Titles . . .

MINISTERS OF GOD, MINISTERS OF THE PEOPLE
Testimonies of Faith from Nicaragua
by Teófilo Cabestrero

Teófilo Cabestrero, a Spanish priest-journalist now working in Nicaragua, presents extensive and exclusive interviews with Ernesto Cardenal, Minister of Culture, Fernando Cardenal, Youth Movement Coordinator, and Miguel d'Escoto, Foreign Minister. These three priests in the Nicaraguan government explain how they combine their priesthood and their political commitment.

"The gift of this book is in the intimate nature of its sharing."   *Sojourners*

no. 335-X   160pp. pbk. $6.95

THE RELIGIOUS ROOTS OF REBELLION
Christians in Central American Revolutions
by Phillip Berryman

A well-documented history and analysis of Christian involvement in revolutionary movements in Nicaragua, El Salvador, and Guatemala.

"This is a provocative and important contribution to understanding the role of Catholicism in the struggle for justice in Central America."   *Penny Lernoux*

Phillip Berryman spent more than a decade in Central America, first as a pastoral worker in a barrio in Panama, and later as Central American representative for the American Friends Service Committee.

no. 105-5   480pp. pbk. $19.95

ARCHBISHOP ROMERO
Martyr of Salvador
by Plácido Erdozaín
Foreword by Jorge Lara-Braud

"It is a compelling, at times emotional, and fast moving book that shows Romero's conversion from a traditional ecclesiastic to an active believer in liberation theology."   *Journal of Church and State*

Plácido Erdozaín is an Augustinian priest who worked closely with Archbishop Romero in San Salvador.

no. 019-9   128pp. pbk. $4.95

SOLIDARITY WITH THE PEOPLE OF NICARAGUA
by James McGinnis

One of the authors of Parenting for Peace and Justice (Orbis 1981) spells out what it means to link our lives with the struggling people of Nicaragua. James McGinnis describes in detail most of the major U.S. Nicaraguan solidarity projects, including "Playgrounds not Battlegrounds," "Medical Aid for Nicaragua," and "Witness for Peace." Each chapter illustrates some aspect of Nicaraguan life and the post-revolutionary process of national reconstruction.

"An excellent combination of resources, analysis, and reflection."
Jim Wallis, Sojourners

James McGinnis, who has made two journeys to Nicaragua, is a staff member of the Institute for Peace and Justice in St. Louis.

no. 448-8   192pp. pbk. $7.95

BLOOD OF THE INNOCENT
Victims of the Contras' War in Nicaragua
edited by Teofilo Cabestrero

In this alarming volume, witnesses and survivors of contra assaults on Nicaraguan peasants recount their horrifying experiences. They tell stories of campesino leaders slaughtered for their efforts to aid peasants, women and children forced to witness the murders of members of their own family and then robbed of all their possessions, the brutal slayings of unarmed children and a defenseless, severely retarded man, and the destruction of cooperative communities in which peasants lived and worked to provide food, housing, and education for each other. These are just some of the startling and disturbing accounts presented here. But equally disturbing is the question that is asked time and again throughout the book: "Why does the United States continue to support this aggression?

Teofilo Cabestrero, a Spanish priest and journalist, is the author of Faith: Conversations With Contemporary Theologians, Mystic of Liberation, and Ministers of God, Ministers of the People, all published by Orbis.

no. 211-6   112pp. pbk. $6.95

SANCTUARY
The New Underground Railroad
by Renny Golden and Michael McConnell

Sanctuary: The New Underground Railroad tells the story of the Sanctuary Movement and its unparalleled grassroots impact on the North American religious community. Written from the perspective of those who have lived it, each chapter begins with a refugee story pulling the reader into the courage of Central Americans struggling for life in the midst of atrocity. The authors, poets and storytellers, take the reader on a clandestine trip along the new underground railroad, showing the world through the eyes of a campesino looking toward El Norte.

"This book is both heart-wrenching and spine-stiffening. These are stories of cruelty inflicted on innocent people by U.S. terrorists that make one weep. But the same stories communicate the courage of the innocent in ways that demand response. . . . Our own spines can be stiffened if we allow some of their courage to rub off on us."

Robert McAfee Brown

Renny Golden and Michael McConnell, members of the Chicago Religious Task Force on Central America, have been "conductors" on the underground railroad since its inception. They have published several articles on Sanctuary and Central America in *Christianity and Crisis, U.S.A. Today, The National Catholic Reporter, Sojourners, The Chicago Tribune, The Other Side,* and the *Witness.*

no. 440–2   **240pp. pbk.**   **$7.95**

LATIN AMERICA AND CARIBBEAN
A Directory of Resources
compiled and edited by Thomas P. Fenton and Mary J. Heffron

In *Latin America and Caribbean* the authors offer hundreds of resources, including organizations, books, periodicals, pamphlets and articles, films, slide shows and videotapes. The result is a set of comprehensive reference tools that will be of use to students, educators, researchers, and church and political activists.

Thomas Fenton and Mary Heffron are currently staff members of the Data Center, a public-interest information library in Oakland, California.

no. 529–8   **144p. pbk**   **$9.95**

STEADFASTNESS OF THE SAINTS
A Journal of Peace and War in Central and North America
by Daniel Berrigan

In this poignant and beautifully written account of his recent journey through Nicaragua and El Salvador, Daniel Berrigan attempts to respond, both as a U.S. citizen and as a Jesuit, to the horrors of the U.S.-supported aggression against the peoples of Central America.

"Daniel Berrigan looks at Central America from the perspective of 'our' America and his new book is written from both sides of the fence. The victimizers are seen through the eyes of the victims. He never loses sight of the interrelation between Megadeath, made in the U.S.A., and the mutilated corpses of children in El Salvador." *Dorothee Soelle*

Daniel Berrigan is a Jesuit and ardent social activist.

no. 447–X   **144pp. pbk.**   **$7.95**